W9-CQS-666

World War I

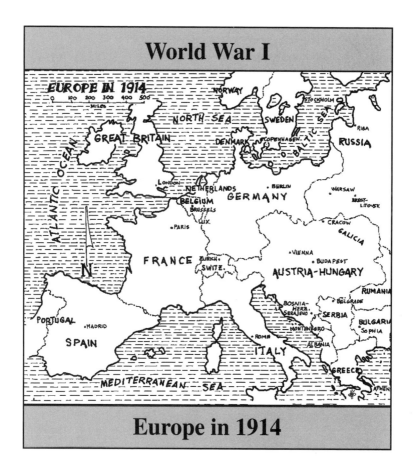

EUROPE IN 1914
0 100 200 300 400 500
MILES

NORWAY

STOCKHOLM

NORTH SEA

SWEDEN

RIGA

RUSSIA

GREAT BRITAIN

DENMARK

COPENHAGEN

ATLANTIC OCEAN

LONDON

NETHERLANDS

BERLIN

WARSAW

BELGIUM

GERMANY

BREST-LITOVSK

BRUSSELS

LUX.

CRACOW

PARIS

GALICIA

N

FRANCE

ZURICH

SWITZ.

VIENNA

BUDAPEST

AUSTRIA-HUNGARY

RUMANIA

BELGRADE

BOSNIA-HERZ.

SERAJEVO

SERBIA

PORTUGAL

MADRID

MONTENEGRO

BULGARIA

SOPHIA

SPAIN

ROME

ALBANIA

ITALY

GREECE

MEDITERRANEAN SEA

ATHENS

Europe in 1914

.."a passionate attachment of one nation for another produces a variety of evils. Sympathy for the favorite nation, facilitating the illusion of an imaginary common interest in cases where no real common interest exists, and infusing into one the enmities of the other, betrays the former into a participation in the quarrels and wars of the latter, without adequate inducement or justification. It leads also to concession to the favorite nation of privileges denied to others, which is apt doubly to injure the nation making the concessions; by unnecessarily parting with what ought to have been retained; and by exciting jealousy, ill-will and a disposition to retaliate, in the parties from whom equal privileges are withheld. And it gives to ambitious, corrupted or deluded citizens (who devote themselves to the favorite nation) facility to betray, or sacrifice the interests of their own country, without odium, sometimes even with popularity .... Against the insidious wiles of foreign influence, (I conjure you to believe me fellow-citizen) the jealousy of a free people ought to be constantly awake."

— George Washington

WASHINGTON'S FAREWELL ADDRESS, 1796

"I have ever deemed it fundamental for the United States never to take active part in the quarrels of Europe. Their political interests are entirely distinct from ours. Their mutual jealousies, their balance of power, their complicated alliances, their forms and principles of government, are all foreign to us. They are nations of eternal war."

— Thomas Jefferson, 1823

"Never was so much false arithmetic employed on any subject, as that which has been employed to persuade nations that it is in their interest to go to war."

— Thomas Jefferson, 1782

About the Uncle Eric Series

The Uncle Eric series of books is written by Richard J. Maybury for young and old alike. Using the epistolary style of writing (using letters to tell a story), Mr. Maybury plays the part of an economist writing a series of letters to his niece or nephew. Using stories and examples, he gives interesting and clear explanations of topics that are generally thought to be too difficult for anyone but experts.

Mr. Maybury warns, "beware of anyone who tells you a topic is above you or better left to experts. Many people are twice as smart as they think they are, but they've been intimidated into believing some topics are above them. You can understand almost anything if it is explained well."

The series is called UNCLE ERIC'S MODEL OF HOW THE WORLD WORKS. In the series, Mr. Maybury writes from the political, legal and economic viewpoint of America's Founders. The books can be read in any order, and have been written to stand alone. To get the most from each one, however, Mr. Maybury suggests the following order of reading:

Uncle Eric's Model
of How the World Works

Uncle Eric Talks About Personal, Career, and Financial Security

Whatever Happened to Penny Candy?

Whatever Happened to Justice?

Are You Liberal? Conservative? or Confused?

Ancient Rome: How It Affects You Today

Evaluating Books: What Would Thomas Jefferson Think About This?

The Money Mystery

The Clipper Ship Strategy

The Thousand Year War in the Mideast

World War I: The Rest of the Story and How It Affects You Today

World War II: The Rest of the Story and How It Affects You Today

(Study guides available or forthcoming for above titles.)

An Uncle Eric Book

World War I

The Rest of the Story
and How It Affects You Today
1870 to 1935

Revised Edition

Part one of a two-part series about the World Wars

by Richard J. Maybury
(Uncle Eric)

published by
Bluestocking Press
www.BluestockingPress.com

Copyright © 2003 by Richard J. Maybury
Previous edition copyrighted © 2002 by Richard J. Maybury
All rights reserved. No part of this transcript may be reproduced or
transmitted in any form or by any means, electronic or mechanical,
including photocopying, recording or by any informational storage or
retrieval system, except by a reviewer who may quote brief passages in
a review to be printed in a magazine or newspaper, without permission
in writing from the author or publisher. Although the author and publisher
have researched all sources to ensure the accuracy and completeness of
the information contained in this book, we assume no responsibility for
errors, inaccuracies, omissions or any inconsistency herein. Any slights
of people or organizations are unintentional.

Printed and bound in the United States of America.
Cover illustrations by Bob O'Hara, Georgetown, CA
Cover design by Brian C. Williams, El Dorado, CA
Edited by Jane A. Williams
          Library of Congress Cataloging-in-Publication Data
Maybury, Rick.
    World War I : the rest of the story and how it affects you today, 1870
to 1935 / by Richard J. Maybury ; [edited by Jane A. Williams].-- Rev. ed.
        p. cm. -- (An Uncle Eric book)
"Part one of a two-part series about the World Wars."
Summary: An examination of the ideas and events that led to World War I,
events during the war, and how they led to World War II, written as a series
of letters from a man to his niece or nephew.
Includes bibliographical references and index.
        ISBN-13: 978-0-942617-42-9
        ISBN-10: 0-942617-42-8
    1. World War, 1914-1918--Causes--Juvenile literature. 2. World War,
1914-1918--United States--Juvenile literature. 3. World War, 1914-1918--
Diplomatic history--Juvenile literature. 4. World War, 1914-1918--
Influence--Juvenile literature. 5. Europe--History--1871-1918--Juvenile
literature. [1. World War, 1914-1918. 2. Europe--History--1871-1918.]
I. Title: World War 1, the rest of the story and how it affects you today,
1870 to 1935. II. Title: World War One, the rest of the story and how it
affects you today, 1870 to 1935. III. Williams, Jane A., 1950- IV. Title. V.
Series.
    D511.M323 2003
    940.3--dc22   2003016764
Published by Bluestocking Press • P.O. Box 1014
Placerville, CA 95667-1014
web site: www.BluestockingPress.com

To the independent thinkers who refuse to march off to war until they fully understand the opponent's point of view, and only after they have seen a mountain of evidence that the war is for an extremely good reason.

"...the entire [Uncle Eric] series should be a required, integral, component of the social studies curriculum in all public and private schools. This would bring a quantum leap upward in the quality of citizenship in this country in a single generation."

—William P. Snavely
Emeritus Professor of Economics
George Mason University

Uncle Eric's Model of How the World Works

What is a model? In his book UNCLE ERIC TALKS ABOUT PERSONAL, CAREER, AND FINANCIAL SECURITY, Richard Maybury (Uncle Eric) explains that one of the most important things you can teach children or learn yourself is:

"Models are how we think, they are how we understand how the world works. As we go through life we build these very complex pictures in our minds of how the world works, and we're constantly referring back to them — matching incoming data against our models. That's how we make sense of things.

"One of the most important uses for models is in sorting incoming information to decide if it's important or not.

"In most schools, models are never mentioned because the teachers are unaware of them. One of the most dangerous weaknesses in traditional education is that it contains no model for political history. Teachers teach what they were taught — and no one ever mentioned models to them, so they don't teach them to their students.

"For the most part, children are just loaded down with collections of facts that they are made to memorize. Without good models, children have no way to know which facts are important and which are not. Students leave school thinking history is a senseless waste of time. Then, deprived of the real lessons of history, the student is vulnerable."

The question is, which models to teach. Mr. Maybury says, "The two models that I think are crucially important for everyone to learn are economics and law."

WHATEVER HAPPENED TO PENNY CANDY? explains the economic model, which is based on Austrian economics, the most free-market of all economic models. WHATEVER HAPPENED TO JUSTICE? explains the legal model and shows the connection between rational law and economic progress. The legal model is the old British Common Law — or Natural Law. The original principles on which America was founded were those of the old British Common Law.

These two books, PENNY CANDY and JUSTICE, provide the overall model of how human civilization works, especially the world of money.

Once the model is understood, read ARE YOU LIBERAL? CONSERVATIVE? OR CONFUSED? This book explains political philosophies relative to Uncle Eric's Model — and makes a strong case for consistency to that model, no exceptions.

Next, read ANCIENT ROME: HOW IT AFFECTS YOU TODAY, which shows what happens when a society ignores Uncle Eric's Model and embraces fascism—an all too common practice these days, although the word fascism is never used.

To help you locate books and authors generally in agreement with these economic and legal models, Mr. Maybury wrote EVALUATING BOOKS: WHAT WOULD THOMAS

JEFFERSON THINK ABOUT THIS? This book provides guidelines for selecting books that are consistent with the principles of America's Founders. You can apply these guidelines to books, movies, news commentators, and current events — to any spoken or written medium.

Further expanding on the economic model, THE MONEY MYSTERY explains the hidden force affecting your career, business, and investments. Some economists refer to this force as velocity, others to money demand. Whichever term is used, it is one of the least understood forces affecting your life. Knowing about velocity and money demand not only gives you an understanding of history that few others have, it prepares you to understand and avoid pitfalls in your career, business, and investments. THE MONEY MYSTERY is the first sequel to WHATEVER HAPPENED TO PENNY CANDY? It provides essential background for getting the most from THE CLIPPER SHIP STRATEGY.

THE CLIPPER SHIP STRATEGY explains how government's interference in the economy affects business, careers, and investments. It's a practical nuts-and-bolts strategy for prospering in our turbulent economy. This book is the second sequel to WHATEVER HAPPENED TO PENNY CANDY? and should be read after THE MONEY MYSTERY.

THE THOUSAND YEAR WAR IN THE MIDEAST: HOW IT AFFECTS YOU TODAY explains how events on the other side of the world a thousand years ago can affect us more than events in our own hometowns today. In the last quarter of the 20th century, the Thousand Year War has been the cause of great shocks to the investment markets — the oil embargoes, the Iranian hostage crisis, the Iraq-Kuwait war, the Caucasus Wars over the Caspian Sea oil basin, and September 11th — and it is likely to remain so for decades to come. Forewarned is forearmed. You must understand where this war is leading to manage your career, business, and investments.

The explosion of the battleship Maine in Havana Harbor in 1898 was the beginning of a chain reaction that eventually led to the destruction of the World Trade Center. In his two-part World War series Richard Maybury explains that an unbroken line leads directly from the Spanish-American War through World War I, World War II, the Korean and Vietnam Wars, the Iraq-Kuwait War, and the "War on Terror" that began September 11, 2001. Mr. Maybury explains the other side of the story, the side you are not likely to get anywhere else, in this two-part World War series: WORLD WAR I: THE REST OF THE STORY AND HOW IT AFFECTS YOU TODAY and WORLD WAR II: THE REST OF THE STORY AND HOW IT AFFECTS YOU TODAY.

Uncle Eric's Model
of How the World Works

These books can be read in any order and have been written to stand alone. But to get the most from each one, Mr. Maybury suggests the following order of reading:

Book 1. UNCLE ERIC TALKS ABOUT PERSONAL, CAREER, AND FINANCIAL SECURITY.
Uncle Eric's Model introduced. Models (or paradigms) are how people think; they are how we understand our world. To achieve success in our careers, investments, and every other part of our lives, we need sound models. These help us recognize and use the information that is important and bypass that which is not. In this book, Mr. Maybury introduces the model he has found most useful. These are explained in WHATEVER HAPPENED TO PENNY CANDY? WHATEVER HAPPENED TO JUSTICE? and THE CLIPPER SHIP STRATEGY.

Book 2. WHATEVER HAPPENED TO PENNY CANDY? A FAST, CLEAR, AND FUN EXPLANATION OF THE ECONOMICS YOU NEED FOR SUCCESS IN YOUR CAREER, BUSINESS, AND INVESTMENTS.
The economic model explained. The clearest and most interesting explanation of economics around. Learn about investment cycles, velocity, business cycles, recessions, inflation, money demand, and more. Contains "Beyond the Basics," which supplements the basic ideas in the book and is included for readers who choose to tackle more challenging concepts. Recommended by former U.S. Treasury Secretary William Simon and many others.
(Study Guide available.)

Book 3. WHATEVER HAPPENED TO JUSTICE?
The legal model explained. Explores America's legal heritage. Shows what is wrong with our legal system and economy, and how to fix it. Discusses the difference between higher law and man-made law, and the connection between rational law and economic prosperity. Introduces the Two Laws: 1) Do all you have agreed to do. 2) Do not encroach on other persons or their property.

Book 4. ARE YOU LIBERAL? CONSERVATIVE? OR CONFUSED?
Political labels. What do they mean? Liberal, conservative, left, right, democrat, republican, moderate, socialist, libertarian, communist — what are their economic policies, and what plans do their promoters have for your money? Clear, concise explanations. Facts and fallacies.

Book 5.   **ANCIENT ROME:** HOW IT AFFECTS YOU TODAY.
This book explains what happens when a society
ignores the model. Are we heading for fascism
like ancient Rome? Mr. Maybury uses historical
events to explain current events, including the wars
in the former Soviet Empire, and the legal and
economic problems of America today. With the
turmoil in Russia and Russia's return to fascism,
you must read this book to understand your future.
History does repeat.

Book 6.   **EVALUATING BOOKS:** WHAT WOULD THOMAS JEFFERSON
THINK ABOUT THIS?
Most books, magazines, and news stories are
slanted against the principles of America's
Founders. Often the writers are not aware of it,
they simply write as they were taught. Learn how
to identify the bias so you can make informed
reading, listening, and viewing choices.

Book 7.   **THE MONEY MYSTERY:** THE HIDDEN FORCE AFFECTING
YOUR CAREER, BUSINESS, AND INVESTMENTS.
The first sequel to WHATEVER HAPPENED TO PENNY
CANDY? Some economists refer to velocity, others
to money demand. However it is seen, it is one of
the least understood forces affecting our
businesses, careers, and investments — it is the
financial trigger. This book discusses precautions
you should take and explains why Federal Reserve
officials remain so afraid of inflation. THE MONEY
MYSTERY prepares you to understand and avoid
pitfalls in your career, business, and investments.

Book 8.   THE CLIPPER SHIP STRATEGY: FOR SUCCESS IN YOUR
CAREER, BUSINESS, AND INVESTMENTS.
The second sequel to WHATEVER HAPPENED TO PENNY
CANDY? Conventional wisdom says that when the
government expands the money supply, the money
descends on the economy in a uniform blanket.
This is wrong. The money is injected into specific
locations causing hot spots or "cones" such as the
tech bubble of the 1990s. Mr. Maybury explains
his system for tracking and profiting from these
cones. Practical nuts-and-bolts strategy for
prospering in our turbulent economy.

Book 9.   THE THOUSAND YEAR WAR IN THE MIDEAST: HOW IT
AFFECTS YOU TODAY.
Mr. Maybury shows that events on the other side
of the world a thousand years ago can affect us
more than events in our hometowns today. This
book explains the ten-century battle the U.S. has
entered against the Islamic world. It predicted the
events that began unfolding on September 11,
2001. It helps you understand the thinking of the
Muslims in the Mideast, and why the coming oil
war will affect investment markets around the
globe. In the last three decades this war has been
the cause of great shocks to the economy and
investment markets, including the oil embargoes,
the Iranian hostage crisis, the Iraq-Kuwait war,
the Caucasus Wars over the Caspian Sea oil basin,
and the September 11th attack — and it is likely to
remain so for decades to come. Forewarned is
forearmed. To successfully manage your career,
business, and investments, you must understand
this war.

Book 10. WORLD WAR I: THE REST OF THE STORY AND HOW IT AFFECTS YOU TODAY, 1870 TO 1935.

The explosion of the battleship Maine in Havana Harbor in 1898 was the beginning of a chain reaction that continues today. Mr. Maybury presents an idea-based explanation of the First World War. He focuses on the ideas and events that led to World War I, events during the war, and how they led to World War II. Includes the ten deadly ideas that lead to war.

Book 11. WORLD WAR II: THE REST OF THE STORY AND HOW IT AFFECTS YOU TODAY, 1935 TO SEPTEMBER 11, 2001.

An idea-based explanation of the war. Focuses on events in the Second World War and how our misunderstanding of this war led to America's subsequent wars, including the Korean and Vietnam Wars, the Iraq-Kuwait War, and the "War on Terror" that began September 11, 2001.

Study Guides and/or Tests
are available or forthcoming
for the "Uncle Eric" books.

"Uncle Eric is on my top 10 list of homeschool resources."
—William Cormier
Freelance Writer for homeschool publications

"None of my kids are graduating from high school until they've finished reading all these books. Very highly recommended." (5 hearts)
— Mary Pride
PRACTICAL HOMESCHOOLING MAGAZINE

Quantity Discounts Available

The Uncle Eric books are available at special quantity discounts for bulk purchases to individuals, businesses, schools, libraries, and associations, to be distributed as gifts, premiums, or as fund raisers.

For terms and discount schedule contact:

Special Sales Department
Bluestocking Press
Phone: 800-959-8586
email: CustomerService@BluestockingPress.com
web site: www.BluestockingPress.com

Specify how books are to be distributed: for classrooms, or as gifts, premiums, fund raisers — or to be resold.

Maps

Study Guide Available

BLUESTOCKING GUIDE: WORLD WAR I

by Jane A. Williams

— based on Richard J. Maybury's book —

WORLD WAR I: THE REST OF THE STORY
AND HOW IT AFFECTS YOU TODAY

Includes: 1) chapter-by-chapter comprehension questions and answers for WORLD WAR I: THE REST OF THE STORY, 2) research activities, 3) a list of World War I films, 4) thought questions, and 5) final exam.

Order from your favorite book store or direct from the publisher: Bluestocking Press (see order information on last page of this book).

Study Guides and/or Tests
are available or forthcoming
for other "Uncle Eric" books.

Contents

Note to Reader

Throughout the book, beginning with Chapter One, when a word that appears in the glossary is introduced in the text, it is displayed in **bold typeface.**

Author's Disclosure

For reasons I do not understand, writers today are supposed to be objective. Few disclose the viewpoints or opinions they use to decide what information is important and what is not, or what shall be presented or omitted.

I do not adhere to this standard and make no pretense of being objective. I am biased in favor of liberty, free markets, and international neutrality and proud of it. So I disclose my viewpoint, which you will find explained in detail in my other books.[1]

For those who have not yet read these publications, I call my viewpoint Juris Naturalism (pronounced *jur*-es *nach*-e-re-liz-em, sometimes abbreviated JN) meaning the belief in a natural law that is higher than any government's law. Here are six quotes from America's Founders that help to describe this viewpoint:

> ...all men are created equal, that they are endowed by their Creator with certain unalienable rights.
> — Declaration of Independence, 1776

> The natural rights of the colonists are these: first, a right to life; second to liberty; third to property; together with the right to support and defend them in the best manner they can.
> — Samuel Adams, 1772

---

[1] See Richard Maybury's other Uncle Eric books (see pgs. 8-15), published by Bluestocking Press, web site: www.BluestockingPress.com

It is strangely absurd to suppose that a million of human beings collected together are not under the same moral laws which bind each of them separately.
— Thomas Jefferson, 1816

A wise and frugal government, which shall restrain men from injuring one another, which shall leave them otherwise free to regulate their own pursuits of industry and improvement, and shall not take from the mouth of labor the bread it has earned. This is the sum of good government.
— Thomas Jefferson, 1801

Not a place on earth might be so happy as America. Her situation is remote from all the wrangling world, and she has nothing to do but to trade with them.
— Thomas Paine, 1776

The great rule of conduct for us, in regard to foreign nations, is, in extending our commercial relations, to have with them as little political connection as possible.
— George Washington, 1796

George
Washington

Cast of Characters

Allies. In both World Wars, the governments of Britain, the U.S. and their allies.

Axis. In World War II, the governments of Germany, Italy, Japan and their lesser allies, principally Bulgaria, Finland, Hungary and Romania. Enemy of the Allies.

Bavaud, Maurice. Swiss theology student who nearly killed Hitler three times between 1938 and his capture and execution in 1941.

Bismark, Otto von. Highly influential German leader in later half of the 19th century. Died in 1898, but his dream for a powerful Germany was a guiding light for Germans in both World Wars. Symbolizing his importance, in World War II an unusually powerful German battleship was named after him.

Central Powers. In World War I, the government of Germany and its allies, principally Austria-Hungary, Bulgaria and Turkey.

Churchill, Winston. Prime Minister of Britain in World War II. A distant cousin and close friend of U.S. President Franklin Roosevelt. In World War I, Churchill was First Lord of the Admiralty, known as the "father of naval aviation," and served with the army in France. In 1917 he became minister of munitions, concentrating on the production of tanks, which were largely his own brainchild.

Dewey, George. U.S. Admiral. In the Spanish-American War in 1898, destroyed the Spanish fleet in the Philippines, then went on to support U.S. ground troops in the U.S. conquest of the Filipinos. His stunning victories probably helped make Americans overconfident about the amount of blood and treasure they would need to spend to defeat Germany in World War I.

FDR. See listing for Franklin D. Roosevelt.

Hitler, Adolph. German dictator, chief of Nazi Germany in World War II. Corporal in German army in World War I; wounded and temporarily blinded by poison gas, recommended for the Iron Cross award for bravery. Emerged from World War I enraged at Germany's betrayal in the Versailles Treaty.

Kimmel, Husband. U.S. Admiral. Navy commander at Pearl Harbor in 1941; blamed for the disaster at Pearl Harbor. In World War I, Kimmel was aide to Assistant Secretary of the Navy Franklin D. Roosevelt (later President Roosevelt), and served on battleships in European waters.

Mahan, Alfred Thayer. President of the Naval War College in 1890. Wrote three-volume work, THE INFLUENCE OF SEA POWER ON HISTORY, which argued that America needed a strong navy to build a worldwide empire.

McKinley, William. U.S. President, 1897-1901, including the Spanish-American War and conquest of the Philippines.

Mussolini, Benito. Italian dictator, chief of fascist Italy in World War II. Prior to World War I, he was a socialist leader and editor of the socialist newspaper Avanti. During the war he was injured in a training exercise and discharged. At the end of the war he founded the Fascist movement, and in 1922 became head of the Italian government.

Rankin, Jeannette. First woman elected to Congress in 1917. The only legislator to vote against entering both World Wars. Explained that, "I was aware of the falseness of much of the propaganda."

Roosevelt, Franklin D. FDR. U.S. President, 1933-45, including during World War II. Distant cousin of President Theodore Roosevelt. Assistant Secretary of the Navy in World War I.

Roosevelt, Theodore. U.S. President, 1901-1909. Distant cousin of President Franklin D. Roosevelt.

Stalin, Joseph. Soviet dictator, 1924-1953, including during World War II. Responsible for the murder of tens of millions. An ally of President Franklin Roosevelt. A socialist leader prior to World War I, Stalin was a founder of the newspaper Pravda in 1912. Arrested and exiled to Siberia 1913 to 1917. In 1917, he returned to Petrograd and helped lead the socialist revolution that overthrew the Czar and established the Union of Soviet Socialist Republics.

Wilhelm I. First German emperor, 1871 to 1888. Winner of the Franco-Prussian War of 1870.

Wilson, Woodrow. U.S. President, 1913-1921, including during World War I.

USG. United States Government.

Timeline

Franco-Prussian War

Alfred Thayer Mahan
writes "Influence of
Seapower upon History"

German
nation
established

Spanish-American War

U.S. Conquest of
Philippines

U.S. takes
Panama from
Columbia

Great White Fleet

World War I

Treaty of
Versailles

World War II

Korean War

Vietnam War

Iraq-
Kuwait
War

World
Trade
Center
destroyed

1870 1880 1890 1900 1910 1920 1930 1940 1950 1960 1970 1980 1990 2000

1

The 58-Year Persecution

Dear Chris,

Thanks for your recent letter. You said you are studying the Second World War, but you suspect there is more to the story than what your history book is telling.

You asked for my perspective on World War II, Admiral Kimmel, General Short,[2] and the attack on Pearl Harbor.

Chris, in order to address your questions and concerns completely, I will need to write you a series of letters so that you can fully understand the story. I will begin with events leading not to World War II but to World War I because my research and study have caused me to view World War II as chapter two of World War I.

If you find this surprising, you are not alone. I'm sure most Americans have never thought of the wars this way. Connections in political and economic history are seldom taught in schools. Subjects are compartmentalized. Educators tend to teach as they were taught and most of them were taught the same compartmentalized approach to history. The lack of connections, as well as the lack of economic history, reinforces a student's tendency to have an oversimplified view of the World Wars and, indeed, of all wars.

---

[2] Admiral Kimmel and General Short were the commanders at Pearl Harbor when the Japanese navy attacked on December 7, 1941.

In other words, you cannot understand World War II and the events that have grown out of it — including September 11, 2001[3] — unless you understand World War I and the ideas and events that led to it. That is my opinion; all these incidents are part of the same story.

The common thread that runs through the whole tapestry will be no surprise to you. I have written about it often in my previous set of letters to you on the subject of justice.[4] Two legal principles make peace, liberty, and prosperity possible. Where these principles are widely violated, life gets worse, and where they are widely obeyed, life gets better.

The first, do all you have agreed to do, is the basis of contract law.

The second, do not encroach on other persons or their property, is the basis of tort law and some criminal law.

These are the two laws taught by all religions.

Each religion phrases them differently, but all teach these two laws. This is the point where all religions come together, the common ground, which is why these laws were the basis of the old British Common Law.

Governments — dozens of them — violate these laws endlessly, and each violation helps set the stage for new disasters, which then become the excuse for more violations.

Chris, as I see it, what Americans have been taught about the World Wars is one of the great falsehoods in history.

---

[3] On September 11, 2001, in an attack against the United States, over 3000 civilians were murdered. The World Trade Center in New York was destroyed, as well as a portion of the Pentagon. Four civilian airliners were destroyed, including their passengers and crew. This attack is also referred to as Sept. 11, Sept. 11 Attack, and 9-11.

[4] Uncle Eric is referring to Richard J. Maybury's book WHATEVER HAPPENED TO JUSTICE? published by Bluestocking Press, web site: www.BluestockingPress.com

Americans have been given facts that have been carefully selected to paint a picture of the U.S. Government as hero and savior of the world. Facts tending to counter this hero and savior image have been buried. (By the way, if you haven't read it already, I highly recommend the excellent book HOW TO LIE WITH STATISTICS[5] by Darrell Huff. Professor Huff shows how the omission of a few seemingly insignificant statistics can seriously distort our understanding.)

For thirty years I have been researching the two World Wars. The additional facts are revealing and paint an entirely different picture.

For instance, Kimmel and Short are generally blamed for the disaster at Pearl Harbor. Americans have been taught that these men had been warned to be ready for an attack, but neglected to prepare, and their forces were caught by surprise.

You might be interested to know that after 58 years of blame, Kimmel and Short were officially declared innocent. The U.S. Senate looked at the evidence and on May 25, 1999, voted that Kimmel and Short had performed their duties "competently and professionally" and the losses at Pearl Harbor were "not the result of dereliction of duty."[6]

Imagine, Chris, for 58 years these men and their families were persecuted unjustly; it took the government that long to own up to its mistake. In my next set of letters about World War II,[7] you will get the facts that were buried for

---

[5] Uncle Eric is referring to the book HOW TO LIE WITH STATISTICS by Darrell Huff, published by W.W. Norton, New York, 1982.

[6] "Pearl Harbor: Senate Clears Kimmel and Short," NEW AMERICAN, July 6, 1999.

[7] Uncle Eric is referring to Richard Maybury's book, WORLD WAR II: THE REST OF THE STORY AND HOW IT AFFECTS YOU TODAY, (part two of a two-part world war series) published by Bluestocking Press, web site: www.BluestockingPress.com

more than a half-century. This is only one example of deceit that has grown out of the official story about the World Wars.

Among other things, what we have been taught about World War II has shifted blame for the U.S. involvement from the politicians to military officers. If Kimmel and Short had been prepared, we were told, the Japanese would have been beaten at Pearl Harbor, and the war might have ended on the first day.

These distortions are highly important because what we think happened in the past determines the decisions we make today and in the future.

What Americans thought happened in World War I determined the decisions they made about World War II.

I believe our misunderstandings about the World Wars have led America into many other foreign conflicts and other kinds of serious trouble. These misunderstandings have caused American individuals to support the government's mistakes, and to go along with these mistakes, sometimes even to the point of risking their lives and dying for them.

Chris, please pay close attention to what I will say in this set of letters about World War I. I am writing them to you so that you do not make uninformed choices, as did so many from my generation — including myself.

I will not give you a highly detailed chronology of the World Wars. You can get that from any encyclopedia, television (especially the History Channel), screenplays, as well as thousands of books and articles that are available in public libraries. My purpose here is not to repeat what you can easily find in these other sources, but to give you a way to understand it, to sort the wheat from the chaff.

My approach will be to give you what you will rarely get elsewhere, not a description of the wars but an *explanation*.

I want you to *understand* the wars.

I will fill in a lot of blanks and you will experience some remarkable facts.

As usual, I admit to you up front that my presentation will not be objective. My observations and conclusions are based on the principles taught by Thomas Jefferson and the other American Founders. Like them, I believe in liberty, free markets, international neutrality, and a government so small you need a microscope to find it. Everything I say will be written from that view — a view you rarely get in other books about the World Wars.

Chris, I want to emphasize, America's Founders believed we must stay neutral in foreign affairs. They also believed that our main system of defense must be the one described in the Second Amendment (and used so effectively by the Swiss for centuries, which I will explain in a future letter). They believed that **political power** corrupts the morals and the judgment — no one can be trusted with it, so the government must be kept very limited.

I think you will find most of what I write about the World Wars interesting, but some may be shocking. When talking about events that brutally killed tens of millions, the horror is impossible to avoid. I will try to keep it to a minimum.

In order to give the rest of the story that you are not likely to get anywhere else, I will sometimes delve deeply into the **economics**[8] of the World Wars, especially World War II. Economics is rarely touched upon in other history books. Economics reveals many embarrassing truths.

Chris, much of what I say will be critical of the government. Never take this as criticism of America. The

---

[8] Economics is the study of the production and distribution of goods and services.

government and the country are not the same thing. I love America and would not want to live anywhere else, but the government is something else entirely, as we shall see.

Another point. What is patriotism?

Some would say love of country.

Others would say my country right or wrong. This is a shortened version of a remark by U.S. Senator John Jordan Crittenden, who said of the war against Mexico, "I hope to find my country in the right; however, I will stand by her, right or wrong."

In actual practice, my country right or wrong means my government right or wrong. This definition of patriotism leads to doing whatever the government says, even if it is not ethical.

I offer a different definition. To me, **patriotism** means dedication to the *principles* on which the country was founded, and a willingness to stand firm and fight for these principles regardless of what the government says or does.

I like Mark Twain's remark: "My kind of loyalty was loyalty to one's country, not to its institutions or its office holders."

Also, Ralph Waldo Emerson's: "When a whole nation is roaring Patriotism at the top of its voice, I am fain[9] to explore the cleanness of its hands and purity of its heart."

Chris, as you learn more about what really caused the World Wars, you will see why I feel so strongly about the real meaning of patriotism.

Before we get started, I suggest you get the largest, most detailed globe, atlas, or world map that you can find, so that

---

[9] Fain: compelled.

you can more easily follow events as they unfold in my
letters.

Uncle Eric

P.S. Chris, before we move on, a word of caution. None of
what I write should be regarded as an argument for
disarmament or even for weakening America's armed forces.
I believe America should have extremely strong defenses,
but these defenses should be the type intended by America's
Founders — ones designed to protect the country, not to
dominate others. I will explain this in future letters about
Switzerland and the Spanish-American War. Until then, please
keep in mind that I believe in a powerful military defense,
but a type much different than what America has. It would
be entirely fair to say these are anti-war letters written by an
extreme militarist.

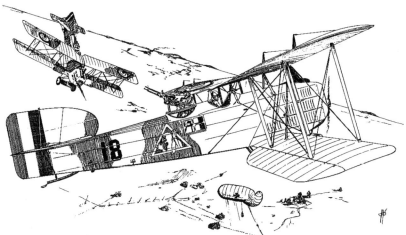

French Breguet 14B-2 Reconnaissance/Bomber. Flown
by Americans by the American Expeditionary Forces 1918.
96th Observation Squadron.

2

The Grim Statistics

Dear Chris,

First things first. War is about death and destruction, so we will get the grimmest of the statistics out of the way now.

No one is sure how many were killed or wounded in the First World War. We do know this war was probably the worst in world history up until that time; only World War II surpassed it.

Here are death estimates from the GROLIER INTERACTIVE ENCYCLOPEDIA and the WORLD ALMANAC.

This is also a revealing list of the chief powers of the two sides, the **Allies** and the **Central Powers.** I suggest you read down the list, locating each country on a globe or world map, so that you have a feel for who was fighting, and who suffered the worst losses.

Incidentally, Chris, the Italian government switched sides, starting the war on the side of the Central Powers and ending on the side of the Allies.

Uncle Eric

World War I Death Estimates

NATION	DEATHS

Chief Allied Powers

Belgium	43,715
British Empire	939,004
France	1,397,800
Greece	137,000
Italy	462,391
Japan	300
Montenegro	3,000
Portugal	100,000
Romania	609,706
Russia	3,700,000
Serbia	695,000
United States	116,708

Chief Central Powers

Austria-Hungary	1,222,500
Bulgaria	350,844
Germany	2,568,546
Turkey	2,475,000

Total Allied dead:	**8,204,624**
Total Central Powers dead:	**6,616,890**
Total dead:	**14,821,514**

U.S. dead as a portion of total dead: 0.3%.

3

Is Now The Time
To Learn About War?

Dear Chris,

The teen years are when the attitudes we have formed about war influence our choices about military service. I know you watch television, so you have already been immersed in the **statist** [10] view of war. Like most others your age, you are encouraged to see war as a contest between the good guys and bad guys.

So the teen years are when it is most important — crucially important — for a person to have the rest of the story, the **non-statist**[11] side, about war.

Chris, I believe wars are rarely about good versus evil, and the World Wars certainly were not. Believing that they were can lead an individual to make uninformed choices — choices that could lead to deadly consequences.

Let me give an example from my own experience. When I was your age, I saw my father and uncles, veterans of World War II, as war heroes, the very definition of what it meant to be a man. All the war movies I watched as a youngster reinforced this image of soldiers as heroes. American soldiers had saved the world from a terrible evil, and I

---

[10] Statist: one who believes in a large, powerful central government, and who believes that there is no law higher than the government's law.

[11] Non-statist: one who believes there is a higher law than any human law, and the government should be subject to this law and kept very limited.

wanted to be like them. I saw military service as my ticket to manhood and spent four years in uniform.

My friends felt this way, too, and this got some of them killed for nothing in Vietnam.

Chris, risking one's life for a hollow cause is not heroism. If I had both sides of the story about the World Wars when I was your age — and if my father and uncles had both sides of the story when they were your age — I wonder how many of us would have risked our lives.

Remember, no politician could go to war unless young men were willing to obey his orders. In exchange, he rewarded them with a uniform, a sign of manhood.

During World War II, Hollywood was hired to promote the hero image through its films. In addition, the marketing and advertising that promoted military service encouraged a young man to see himself as a hero — someone who will save his country from evil. Look at old World War I and World War II recruitment posters. Their message: be a hero.

As World War I and World War II fade into the past, they become more and more wrapped in glory and nobility. Consequently, hearing the rest of the story about the World Wars is more important than ever.

Remember, no matter how much a person thinks he knows about these crucially important events, he cannot be completely informed unless he understands both the non-statist side as well as the statist side.

Chris, in case you have not already guessed, one of my goals in writing these letters is to not only give you the rest of the story about the World Wars, but to cause you to start thinking about war itself. What is it? How does it affect our thinking? Where does it come from?

What does it turn us into?

Uncle Eric

4

First Ideas, Then Battles

Dear Chris,

The usual way to teach about World War I and World War II is to list some of the events leading up to them, then spend most of the effort on the strategies and battles, plus a little about the **diplomacy.**

My letters will try for a deeper understanding, so we need a different approach.

Regarding the effect on the average U.S. citizen today, the strategies and battles of World War I are of limited importance. Highly important, however, are the ideas and events that led to World War I, and to the aftermath that turned out to be World War II.

So most of my letters about the First World War will be about ideas and events which produced that war. The strategies, battles, and diplomacy will get only brief attention.

World War II is the opposite. Its cause is simple — World War I. As I said in an earlier letter, I view the Second World War as chapter two of the First World War; so the most important parts of World War II are the way the U.S. got into it — the attack on Pearl Harbor — and the way the war was conducted. These set the stage for the world we live in today. They affect us profoundly and probably will continue to do so for decades to come. I will spend a lot of ink on them.

So, until we get to the 1930s, we will be talking mostly about ideas and **geopolitical**[12] events. Then in the 1930s, which will begin my next set of letters,[13] we will switch to strategies and battles.

Chris, let me emphasize that, aside from these letters, you will rarely hear much about the *ideas* that led to the World Wars. In my opinion, these are the most important aspects of the whole story, so in this set of letters we will spend a lot of time on them. I'll get to them soon, but I need to cover a few other topics first.

Until then, a key point to remember is that humans have inflicted more than 14,000 wars on themselves,[14] most in the Old World. Both World Wars were typical, garden-variety European and Asian bloodbaths until the U.S. Government (hereafter referred to as the USG) got into them. It was the USG's participation that turned them into World Wars. And this participation did not suddenly spring from nothing. It was the logical result of those ten deadly ideas that lead to war.

To help you better understand the ideas that led to the World Wars, I will choose examples from history with which you are familiar. If it appears that I am putting too much weight on events from World War II, or even contemporary events, in this series of letters about World War I, please be patient. Do you recall what I said in my first letter to you? I

---

[12] Geopolitical: world political events, as opposed to national political events.

[13] When talking about his next set of letters, Uncle Eric is referring to the book WORLD WAR II: THE REST OF THE STORY by Richard J. Maybury, published by Bluestocking Press, web site: www.BluestockingPress.com

[14] DIRTY LITTLE SECRETS, by James F. Dunnigan and Albert A. Nofi, Quill/William Morrow, 1990, p.419.

plan to give you an explanation of the wars, not necessarily a description.

A couple years ago I recommended a book to you called ECONOMICS IN ONE LESSON. Henry Hazlitt, the author, said:

> The whole of economics can be reduced to a single lesson, and that lesson can be reduced to a single sentence.

> The art of economics consists in looking not merely at the immediate but at the longer effects of any act or policy; it consists in tracing the consequences of that policy not merely for one group but for all groups.[15]

To repeat, in order to give the rest of the story about the World Wars, I will sometimes delve deeply into economics. Economics reveals many embarrassing truths. In this set of letters I will, in Hazlitt's words, be *" looking not merely at the immediate but at the longer effects of any act or policy;* [and I will be] *tracing the consequences of that policy not merely for one group but for all groups."*

Until then, remember, there are ten deadly ideas that lead to war, and each idea has a consequence, not merely for one group, but for many groups.

Uncle Eric

P.S. Chris, for the rest of these letters I will be writing a lot about the United States Government. In referring to a national

---

[15] Uncle Eric is referring to the book ECONOMICS IN ONE LESSON by Henry Hazlitt, published by Crown Publishing Group, New York, 1979.

government, writers often use the name of the capital city to show they see a distinction between the government and the country. For example, writers will refer to Moscow instead of Russia, or Washington instead of the United States of America.

When I say Washington, do not think I am referring to George Washington unless I make it clear that I am.

When I write about the United States Government I might refer to Washington D.C., or I will frequently use a more precise term that you may not have seen before: USG, meaning United States Government. Officials in the government often use this term in their internal correspondence to show that they mean the government, not the country.

P.P.S. Also, Chris, I encourage you to examine the footnotes in this set of letters. You will find the research is not from esoteric sources that you cannot check. It's from material that has been freely available to the general public and to historians for years.

All I have done is rearrange and highlight the facts according to my "Uncle Eric Model" which is based on the two laws explained in my previous set of letters on law [WHAT-EVER HAPPENED TO JUSTICE?] — especially, Do not encroach on other persons or their property. This causes the facts to paint a picture much different than the one commonly accepted.

5

Whose Truth?

Dear Chris,

German professor of photography Wilhelm Schurmann points out that a photograph is never **objective**, but always **subjective**. A human being who has feelings and opinions took the photo and wants you to have some kind of reaction to it. "You have to ask, whose truth is being shown," Schurmann warns, and you must always wonder, "What is this photo trying to make me think?"[16]

This series of letters will often use the terms Old World and New World. These terms are seldom used any more, so this map will help fix their meaning in the minds of readers.

---

[16] Quoted by Alexander Smoltczyk in "Der Spiegel," May 24, 1999.

This is good advice, not only for photos, but also for movies, articles, books, and any other form of information, including the letters you are reading now. None are ever objective. Humans produce them, and all humans use some viewpoint to select what they will present and what they will omit.

Always, always, *always,* ask yourself, what is this person trying to make me think? What view did he use to select the information he presents and omits?

It is not customary for a writer to disclose his viewpoint. Generally the reader is left to guess at it. It has been my experience that most writers are statists of one stripe or another, which is why the statist slant is quite common in nearly all history books.

For instance, when you study the creation of the U.S. Government in 1787-90, you usually get only the **Federalist** side of the story. Few Americans realize there was an **anti-Federalist** side that has been nearly erased from our culture.

Also, it used to be when you studied the Civil War, you usually got the North's side. Few Americans ever heard the South's side. It had been erased from our culture. This is changing, especially in many schools in the South.

When you study the World Wars, you get the U.S. Government's side which says America's involvement in the wars was necessary. Few Americans ever hear the other side. You will. But first, I want to recommend two films that are superb examples of the government's explanation of why Americans should support the World Wars. I will tell you more about them in my next letter.

Uncle Eric

6

Why We Fight

Dear Chris,

In World War II, the Federal Government wanted a series of films that would explain why Americans should support the fight. Officials asked Frank Capra to do it, and the result was the series WHY WE FIGHT.

Capra is justifiably famous for his ability to make movies that touch the hearts of Americans and give new ways to view the world. His movie IT'S A WONDERFUL LIFE, starring James Stewart, is a classic.

The message in WHY WE FIGHT is that America is good, and because it is good it has the duty to send its young men and women to risk their lives fighting evil anywhere in the world.

WHY WE FIGHT was so persuasive that it became the unquestioned explanation of *both* World Wars. Its view saturates nearly everything Americans have written about the wars, and even today millions who have never heard of WHY WE FIGHT believe its message as the whole truth because that message is still so widely taught. I highly recommend that you watch WHY WE FIGHT.

WHY WE FIGHT paved the way for the second source, the 1954 television series VICTORY AT SEA produced by Henry Salomon.

Both film series gave a Hollywood view of the wars. The Germans were the bad guys and the Americans the good guys (typical good guy vs. bad guy movie plot). That was the total explanation for both World Wars, good guys against bad guys, and it is still widely believed today.

VICTORY AT SEA was broadcast in the decade when television was new and there were only three TV networks, so a uniformity of viewing experience existed from coast to coast. Everyone knew who Ed Sullivan, Lucille Ball, and Howdy Doody were, and could go to work on Monday morning certain about the topics of conversation that would arise from their weekend viewing.

If you are able to watch WHY WE FIGHT and VICTORY AT SEA, pay close attention to your emotions aroused by the music. What are you feeling?

Music is an important part of any movie experience. It creates the film's emotions. It subconsciously tells you what to think and feel about the images on the screen. Music burrows deep into your soul and persuades, often without the viewer knowing he has been persuaded.

With a stirring musical score by master composer Richard Rodgers, VICTORY AT SEA gave the entire American population an in-depth exposure to the **propaganda**[17] in WHY WE FIGHT. The VICTORY AT SEA television series is a must. If you do not have the time to watch all 26 segments, they have been compressed into a two-hour movie often shown on television. Ask for them at a local video store or library.

Please, Chris, if you can possibly find copies of them, watch WHY WE FIGHT and VICTORY AT SEA. They will give you a quick yet profound understanding of why Americans believe what they do about the World Wars.

---

[17] Propaganda: strongly biased information designed to persuade, usually relating to political or economic matters. The bias is often subtle and usually hidden and may make use of lies and half-truths.

In addition, a complete understanding of the World Wars requires you to have a full understanding of the official side, meaning the government's side. Thousands of books and probably hundreds of movies give this view, but a quicker, more revealing and entertaining way to get the official story is to go straight to these two original film sources.

These movies give what I call "the Hollywood history" of the war, which is also the government's history. For the rest of these letters to you I will refer to "the Hollywood view" as the view approved by the government and shown in WHY WE FIGHT and VICTORY AT SEA.

Both series are almost entirely about World War II, but today we tend to view World War I through the distorted lens of World War II films, so it is important to understand this lens — especially its way of showing the Germans. Many of today's most prominent historians were born between 1930 and 1960, and were deluged by World War II propaganda during their early years. In many cases their work reflects this.

A good supplement to these films is the History Channel's one-hour documentary THE COLOR OF WAR, the segment called "Why We Fight." This is a most revealing look at the thinking of American soldiers, sailors, and airmen in World War II. Among other things, the film explains that in 1942 millions of Americans had no dislike of Germans and many admired them. The government had to use extreme propaganda against Germans so that these millions would hate them. This extreme message still colors our view of both World Wars.

Indeed, propaganda in favor of U.S. involvement in both World Wars was so effective that the attitudes they created are still guiding American **foreign policy** today. Americans support this policy because they still believe the Hollywood view of the World Wars.

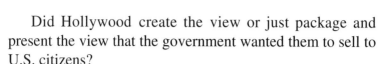

Did Hollywood create the view or just package and present the view that the government wanted them to sell to U.S. citizens?

Both, I think. Many in Hollywood believed the government's view of the wars and were eager to present it. Others were simply paid to do it.

Then after the wars, movies created for entertainment were built on the simplistic "good guys versus bad guys" view. In other words, the war propaganda became a good plot device.

After I write this today, more than a half-century after the World Wars ended, movies and TV shows still use, and therefore reinforce, this simplistic "good guys versus bad guys" view of the world.

Chris, remember the economic lesson referred to earlier. Hazlitt said, *"The art of economics consists in looking not merely at the immediate but at the longer effects of any act or policy; it consists in tracing the consequences of that policy not merely for one group but for all groups."*[18]

The persuasion in WHY WE FIGHT and VICTORY AT SEA has been so effective that for a half-century, publishing a book or producing a movie that disagreed with the official government view was a sure way to lose money. Fortunately, this is changing now that more information about what really happened in the World Wars is leaking out. The Freedom of Information Act that enables scholars to dig into the government's formerly secret files and the computer, make research much easier and effective today.

Chris, if for some reason you cannot watch WHY WE FIGHT and VICTORY AT SEA, you can get the government's official

---

[18] ECONOMICS IN ONE LESSON by Henry Hazlitt, published by Crown Publishing Group, New York, 1979, p 17.

story about the World Wars in any history textbook used in public schools. Public schools are government-owned, so textbook publishers know they have an easier time selling books if they steer clear of any material that might raise the eyebrows of the officials who approve the books. Economics.

Uncle Eric

P.S. Chris, another movie I strongly recommend is THEY WERE EXPENDABLE (1945) starring John Wayne. This is a classic World War II propaganda film aimed at the hearts and minds of young men. I don't want to spoil it for you by revealing the ending, but even at my age, and with all I know about propaganda and war, the movie's ending makes me want to run right down to the nearest recruiter and sign up to fight the Japanese in the Philippines.

You might also take a look at the John Wayne movie SANDS OF IWO JIMA[19] (1949). When marine trainees at Camp Pendleton, California were hired as extras for the 1961 movie THE OUTSIDER about World War II, the director asked them why they had enlisted. Half said it was because they had been inspired by SANDS OF IWO JIMA.[20]

I wonder how many of them survived Vietnam.

---

[19] SANDS OF IWO JIMA was made after World War II but stayed consistent with World War II propaganda, and so had the same effect on young people who saw it years later.

[20] War in the Dark," by Roger J. Spiller, AMERICAN HERITAGE, February/ March 1999, p.41.

7

Conquest Creates Weakness Not Strength

Dear Chris,

If you get the chance to experience WHY WE FIGHT you will see maps showing the **Axis** advance across Europe in World War II. You will be told that as the Axis took more territory it became stronger because it had more slaves and raw materials to make weapons.

This sounds logical but any military officer who has studied the subject will tell you it could not be so.

Taking territory makes an army weaker not stronger.

This myth that taking territory makes an army stronger is the first one we need to erase to understand World War I, or any war.

As an army advances, it must leave troops behind to **occupy** the conquered areas, meaning to watch and control the beaten enemy. The more territory that is taken, the more occupation troops are needed, until finally there are too few troops left to fight at the front lines.

At some point, one more acre of ground will be the straw that breaks the camel's back, and the army will start losing. But no one ever knows which acre that will be. All they know is that as the army advances it becomes weaker.

In World War II, in Yugoslavia alone, the Axis had to station almost 30 **divisions** permanently.[21] This was roughly equal to a third of the forces thrown against the Allies in the invasion of Normandy.

Every conqueror in history has run up against this problem. Troops needed for occupation cannot be available for the front lines. The more territory that is taken, the less can be controlled.

Taking territory creates weakness not strength, but WHY WE FIGHT showed the opposite, and it is still widely believed even among some soldiers who were there and saw the truth with their own eyes.

This myth that taking territory produces strength still hampers our understanding of World War I, World War II, and all other wars. Be on the lookout for it when studying any war. When you see a map of conquered territory, always ask, they took it but can they hold it?

This was a central question in World War I and one of the reasons the war was so awful, as we shall see in a future letter. It led to the "trench warfare" in which hundreds would die trying to hold a single acre of ground.

Incidentally, the weakness caused by taking territory points to a major reason the Soviet Empire fell apart during the late 1980s and early 1990s. The **Kremlin**[22] had taken all the territory it could handle, and when it tried to take Afghanistan in the 1980s, this was the last straw. Putting military forces in Afghanistan meant taking them away from

---

[21] THE RISE AND DECLINE OF THE STATE, by Martin van Creveld, Cambridge University Press, 1999, p.396.

[22] Kremlin: a medieval fortified area in Moscow used as the center of the Russian government. The word is commonly used to mean the Russian government.

other areas. When people in the other areas realized they no longer had anything to fear, the uprisings began, and the empire fell.

Let me emphasize, Chris, that WHY WE FIGHT and VICTORY AT SEA depict only one view — the statist view — of World War II, and this has led to the same single view of World War I. Watch these films not to learn history but to learn what most Americans *think* is history.

Remember, Chris, taking more territory creates weakness not strength.

Uncle Eric

P.S. Incidentally, Chris, keep that rule in mind when reading the daily newspaper. In the 1990s, the U.S. Government adopted as part of its foreign policy the belief that U.S. troops should be "peacekeepers" sent to occupy other lands to keep warring groups from killing each other. The idea sounded good, but in the long run it turned out that the more American troops were used to occupy foreign lands, the fewer were available to defend America. On September 11th, dozens of foreign rulers were better protected by American troops than were the people of New York City.

8

Typical Garden-Variety Wars

Dear Chris,

I spent four years in the Air Force during the 1960s, and the main thing I learned is that I did not know anything about real history or real politics.

Knowing what I know now, the only American war I would ever have volunteered for was the 1776 American Revolution. All the others, as far as I have been able to tell, have been the result of U.S. officials interfering in other people's business. By the time we finish these letters about World War I and World War II[23] you will know why I say that.

The World Wars were typical garden-variety European and Asian bloodbaths — the same horror that has been going on in the Old World for thousands of years. They did not become World Wars until the USG got into them. And the USG was not on the side of the good guys.

There were no good guys.

Hitler was horrifically evil, true, and so were the rulers of Japan and Italy. But President Franklin D. Roosevelt's ally Joseph Stalin was worse than the other three combined. I will spend several letters giving you the facts about this.

---

[23] Uncle Eric is referring to this set of letters about WORLD WAR I as well as Richard J. Maybury's book WORLD WAR II: THE REST OF THE STORY, which is part two in Maybury's World War series, published by Bluestocking Press, web site: www.BluestockingPress.com

The government of Britain, another ally of the USG, was not a group of choirboys, either, nor were the USG's allies in World War I.

The propaganda about World War II has led many to believe World War I was the same kind of contest, good guys against bad guys, with Berlin being the scourge of the world.

Berlin was not a collection of saints and angels in either war, but neither were Moscow, London, or the other governments fighting Berlin.

To measure the extent of the evil these people committed, I will use body counts. The number of innocent people murdered seems one of the most revealing ways to measure evil. In a letter about World War II, we will look at the body counts of the various players. I am sure you will be amazed.

In World War II, the group of countries led by Germany, Italy, and Japan was called the Axis. The group led by the U.S., Britain, and Russia was called the Allies.

In World War I the Allies included: France, Russia, Great Britain, the U.S., Japan, Italy, China, and Brazil. The Central Powers consisted of Germany, the Austro-Hungarian Empire, Turkey, and Bulgaria.

In my view, neither side was good in World War I or World War II, which is why the USG should have stayed out.

I repeat, these were typical garden-variety European and Asian wars, the same kind of insanity these Old World governments have been engaged in for thousands of years. The scale of the death and destruction was greater due to the advanced weapons, but that was the only important difference. These were certainly not fights between good and evil, as Americans have been taught.

Uncle Eric

9

Deadly Ideas Lead to War

Dear Chris,

War is not some kind of natural disaster like a storm or earthquake; it is a form of human behavior.

Humans behave the way they do because they think the way they do.

To understand a war, you must understand the ideas that lead to this behavior.

In other words, Chris, war is something humans *choose* to do because of the *ideas* they hold.

The ideas that got America into the World Wars did not suddenly spring up in 1917 or 1941. The ideas developed slowly over thousands of years.

In the next few letters I will detail what I believe are the ten deadly ideas that lead to war. I have listed them for you at the end of this letter.

We can trace these deadly ideas back at least as far as the Roman Empire. So let's get started examining all this. When you understand the ten deadly ideas, you will understand how World War I happened.

Uncle Eric

The Ten Deadly Ideas That Lead to War

1. The Pax Romana

2. Fascism

3. Love of political power

4. Global protection

5. Interests

6. Cost externalization

7. Manifest Destiny

8. The White Man's Burden (or Anglo-Saxonism)

9. Alliances

10. The glory of war

10

The Pax Romana

Dear Chris,

Do you remember my previous set of letters about ANCIENT ROME?[24] In those letters you learned that for two thousand years the world's chief powers, which means mostly the European powers, have been dominated by the idea of the **Pax Romana**.

Pax is the Latin word for peace. The Pax Romana myth says that for two centuries, beginning in 31 B.C., the Roman Empire was peaceful and prosperous due to a huge, powerful central government that kept everyone in line. *The Pax Romana is the first deadly idea that leads to war.*

European statists pine for a return to the Pax Romana, never mind that it did not happen. The 200-year "pax" was filled with tyranny, assassinations, terror, rebellions, foreign wars, and civil wars. The Hebrew revolt in 70 A.D. was only one of the better-known bloody incidents throughout the Roman Empire during that period.

The Roman "peace" was horrific, but the legend stuck, and today few question the need for a strong central government that dominates everyone.

---

[24] Uncle Eric is referring to ANCIENT ROME: HOW IT AFFECTS YOU TODAY by Richard J. Maybury, published by Bluestocking Press, web site: www.BluestockingPress.com

Therefore, the Pax Romana is an important idea, perhaps the most important, that has guided the behavior of European rulers for centuries. They believe in the need for a strong central government that dominates everyone. This idea is so important that you might want to go back and review those earlier letters about ANCIENT ROME before reading further.

In my next few letters I will explain more about how Americans were taught the view of the World Wars that they hold today, then we will come back to the Pax Romana, the first deadly idea.

Uncle Eric

11

Fascism

Dear Chris,

The Roman government was strongest in Europe, so Europe is where the Pax Romana myth became most entrenched.

Europe has as many powerseekers as anywhere else, and these powerseekers have never been shy about using the Pax Romana as an excuse to try to conquer as much of the globe as they could.

Chris, after you review my earlier set of letters about ANCIENT ROME, you might get a computer program called CENTENNIA®.[25] This program gives maps and explanations of European history for the past thousand years. The program is so revealing it has been required reading for history students at the U.S. Naval Academy at Annapolis.

Set CENTENNIA® on fast-forward; watch borders change and empires expand and contract as the various Old World governments go to war against each other decade after decade, century after century. You will see why I say that the World Wars were just typical garden-variety European and Asian wars until the USG got into them.

Chris, as you watch this horrific drama unfold, you will notice a recurring pattern. For about nine centuries, the two

---

[25] CENTENNIA® software, PO Box 117, Groton, CT, 06340, web site: www.historicalatlas.com.

dominant powers in Europe were the French Empire and the Austro-Hungarian Empire.[26] Trying to capture as much land and taxpayers as they could, each would surge across Europe, often clashing with the other in the central area between them.

In other words, Denmark, Germany, Switzerland, and Italy were a battleground between these two largest empires.

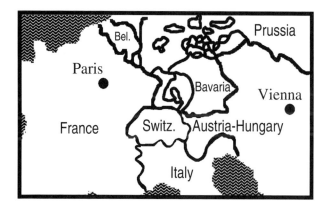

For about nine centuries, Europe was dominated by two competitors, the French Empire and the Austro-Hungarian Empire. (Early versions of the Austro-Hungarian Empire included the Holy Roman Empire and the Habsburg Empire.)

The French government was based in Paris, and the Austro-Hungarian government in Vienna.

The rest of Europe was small states, sometimes hundreds, that often became both the prizes and the battlegrounds in the wars between Paris and Vienna, as shown above in 1870.

Americans have been led to believe that a key feature of European history has been Germany's attempts at conquest, but Germany was a latecomer that was not formed until 1871. The key feature of European history since the Middle Ages has been the feud between the French and Austro-Hungarians, and their conquests of neighboring lands.

---

[26] Early versions of the Austro-Hungarian Empire included the Holy Roman Empire and the Habsburg Empire.

If you ever visit the capitals of the two empires, Paris and Vienna, you will notice many grand buildings decorated with fasces.

As explained in ANCIENT ROME,[27] the fasces was the symbol of the ancient Roman political philosophy called **fascism**.

A **fasces** was a bundle of rods bound with an ax or spear. The bound rods symbolized all the people of all the provinces "unified" under a single government. The ax or spear symbolized what happened to anyone who did not obey this government.

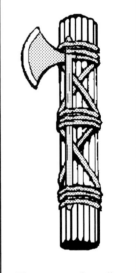

The French and Austro-Hungarian use of fasces in their art and architecture was their way of showing their dedication to fascism — to the attempt to "unify" (conquer) the world under one government in order to create a new Pax Romana.

Fasces: a bundle of rods bound with an ax. It also appears with a spear.

This love of fascism and the Pax Romana was so strong that the fasces is depicted far more in the art and architecture of the modern world than in those of the old Roman Empire. In Vienna, I counted no less than twelve fasces decorating the exterior of the Belvedere Palace.

---

[27] Uncle Eric is referring to Richard J. Maybury's book ANCIENT ROME: HOW IT AFFECTS YOU TODAY, published by Bluestocking Press, web site: www.BluestockingPress.com

Chris, my key point is that fascism was regarded as a respectable philosophy until World War II. You can even find fasces in the art and architecture of America, including the Lincoln Memorial in Washington D.C., completed in 1922. But, in the Second World War, dictators Hitler (Germany) and Mussolini (Italy) showed where fascism leads, so today no one admits to believing in it, and to call a person a fascist is to insult him. The fasces is no longer used in art or architecture.

This does not mean the philosophy is dead — far from it — but the word and symbol are no longer acceptable in polite company.

We are led to believe that fascism popped up suddenly in the 20th century, and World War II was a necessary sacrifice to stop it.

The truth is that fascism was quite popular among Europeans for some two thousand years, and they practiced it widely against each other for many centuries in hopes of creating a new Pax Romana.

Chris, fascism is the second deadly idea that leads to war.

The Italian and German leaders of the Axis were not doing anything new or different; they were just trying to do it more effectively than the French and Austro-Hungarians. This is why Hitler and Mussolini were so popular. Millions all over Europe already believed in what these men would say long before they came to power.

And fascism was as important in World War I as in World War II. It was an old, old habit. Governments on both sides had been killing and conquering for decades, and, in some cases, centuries, spreading their tentacles all the way around the world before World War I.

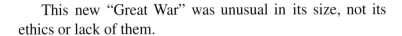

This new "Great War" was unusual in its size, not its ethics or lack of them.

Uncle Eric

P.S. Chris, "The Great War" was one of the original names for World War I. Another was "The World War." After World War II came along, a new name was needed, and today most people say "The First World War" or "World War I."

The Non-ethical Foundation Of Fascism[28]

A quick refresher for those who are too young to remember

Fascists believe that ideas such as right and wrong are for ivory tower intellectuals. What is needed is action.

Right and wrong are just matters of opinion, and they accomplish nothing except to keep men of action from getting the job done.

To a fascist, the only guiding principle is, do whatever appears necessary. No exceptions, no limits.

If free trade appears necessary, we should have free trade. If restrictions on trade appear necessary, we should have restrictions.

If lower taxes appear necessary, that's okay, and if higher taxes appear necessary, that's okay, too.

If freedom appears necessary, fine, and if slavery appears necessary, also fine.

If murdering millions appears necessary, why not? Right and wrong are just matters of opinion.

There is no line a fascist will not cross if he believes it is necessary. This enables a fascist to be a chameleon. On any given issue he will adopt whatever prescription he believes might work. He can appear to be a socialist, a conservative, liberal, libertarian, anything. And if he believes conditions have changed and a new prescription is necessary, he will switch without hesitation.

[28] From Richard Maybury's speech at the Atlanta Investment Conference in April 2001.

12

What Date
Did the World Wars Begin?

Dear Chris,

Thanks for your letter. You asked the exact date when the World Wars began.

That's a tough question. As I said in my last letter, armies swept across the European countryside for centuries fighting for control of land and taxpayers. Each hoped to build a state that would revive the "glory of Rome," and they were willing to do whatever it took to accomplish that.

It is often hard to tell when one war ended and the next began because the goal on both sides was often the same — to be the new Rome — and this goal continued, so fighting rarely died down completely. "Peace" in the Old World was (and mostly still is) just a condition in which there was no fighting at the moment, but all sides were heavily armed and ready to massacre each other at the drop of a hat.

This is why hundreds of European buildings, especially government buildings, are copies of Roman structures. Some have even been given Roman names. The "Pantheon" in Paris, completed in 1790, is a larger version of the ancient Pantheon in Rome built 17 centuries earlier.

The two World Wars of the twentieth century were simply a continuation of European behavior, two more chapters in the ancient attempt to forcibly recreate the Pax Romana.

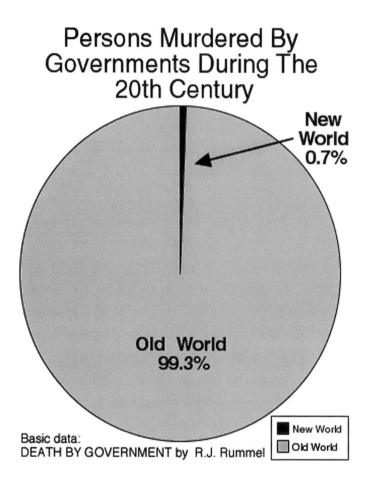

Few Americans realize how bloody the Old World is and always has been. This chart does not show troops or civilians killed in battle, it shows only the unarmed men, women, and children deliberately murdered.

So any answer to your question about the beginning of the World Wars will be rather arbitrary. The only logical starting place is around two thousand years ago in Ancient Rome. The rest has all been downstream from that source. However, I do not want to write the number of letters that would be required to cover two thousand years. You would not get much of additional significance from it, either, because the ideas and behavior changed little, just the weapons and tactics.

Since the Old World's political history is mostly an unvarying tapestry of bloodstains, we could begin the rest of the story about the World Wars almost anywhere. Most historians begin in 1870 with the Franco-Prussian War, and I see no reason not to do the same; so in my next letter I will begin there, too.

Always remember, Chris, that peace has been the exception throughout the Old World. This is why the American Founders advised us to have no political connections with the Old World.

> The great rule of conduct for us, in regard to foreign nations, is in extending our commercial relations, to have with them as little political connection as possible.
>
> — George Washington

> Not a place upon earth might be so happy as America. Her situation is remote from all the wrangling world, and she has nothing to do but to trade with them.
>
> — Thomas Paine

I have ever deemed it fundamental for the United States, never to take active part in the quarrels of Europe. Their political interests are entirely distinct from ours. Their mutual jealousies, their balance of power, their complicated alliances, their forms and principles of government, are all foreign to us. They are nations of eternal war.

— Thomas Jefferson

As to everything except commerce, we ought to divorce ourselves from them all.

— Thomas Jefferson

Notice the Founders did not believe we should be "isolationist." They did not think we should cut ourselves off from the rest of the world. They believed we should visit other countries, be friendly with them, and do business with them — but no political connections, and no involvement in their wars.

Why?

Chris, in 1984, the Norwegian Academy of Sciences and University of Oslo calculated that since the year 3,600 B.C., there had been 14,531 wars.[29] The vast majority were in the Old World.

Since 1984, according to an article in SCIENTIFIC AMERICAN, more than 100 wars have broken out, nearly all in the Old World, and they have killed more than five million.[30]

---

[29] DIRTY LITTLE SECRETS, by James F. Dunnigan and Albert A. Nofi, Quill/William Morrow, 1990, p.419.

[30] "A New Kind Of War," by Jeffrey Boutwell and Michael T. Klare, SCIENTIFIC AMERICAN, June 2000, p.48.

The Founders believed in **neutrality**, or perhaps a better word would be **nonintervention**. Today some confuse this principle with the term **isolationism** to keep voters from giving a policy of nonintervention serious consideration. Let me draw your attention to Jefferson's words about Europe, he called them "nations of eternal war." This is a wonderfully descriptive phrase, and accurate. As I write this, Europe certainly has not cleaned up its act. In the 1990s, war broke out in the European nations of Moldova, Bosnia, Albania, Kosovo, Croatia, Georgia, Armenia, Azerbaijan, Macedonia, and twice in Chechnya. And, beginning the new millennium, war broke out between the USG and groups in the Islamic world. You have read my previous set of letters written before September 11, 2001, about THE THOUSAND YEAR WAR IN THE MIDEAST,[31] so you know this new "War against Terror" is really the latest chapter in a war between Europeans and the Islamic world. It's not an exaggeration to say that the World Trade Center was destroyed in a war that began in Europe ten centuries ago.

Europe gave the world the Thirty Years War, the Hundred Years War, the two World Wars, and a host of others. No other part of the world has shed as much blood as Europe. This is what the Roman philosophy has done.

Uncle Eric

---

[31] Uncle Eric is referring to Richard J. Maybury's book THE THOUSAND YEAR WAR IN THE MIDEAST: HOW IT AFFECTS YOU TODAY, published by Bluestocking Press, web site: www.BluestockingPress.com

13

Franco-Prussian War

Dear Chris,

To a large extent, the history of Europe's wars is a history of shifting **alliances**. For a few years or decades, two or more governments will stand together against a common enemy. Then they will quarrel, divorce, and form new partnerships, often with their former enemies, against their former friends. (As you know, Chris, the USG does the same. In the 1973 and 1979 Arab oil embargoes, the Arab dictators in the Persian Gulf were bankrupting American companies and individuals by restricting the supply of oil and driving up the price. As I write this, these dictators are the USG's allies. In the 1980s, the USG backed Saddam Hussein in his war against Iran. Following September 11th, the USG defined Hussein as an enemy.)

An example from the 1800s was a small power called Prussia. In central Europe on the Baltic, Prussian rulers had been expanding their realm and forming alliances with other powers.

In July 1870, with the encouragement of Prussia's Count Otto von Bismark, Spanish officials offered the Spanish throne to Prince Leopold of the Duchy of Hohenzollern. Leopold was an ally of the Prussians who were enemies of France's Napoleon III.

On July 13th Prussia's King William sent a message to Napoleon III reporting a fairly innocent meeting with the

French ambassador. Bismarck intercepted the telegram and changed it to suggest that the meeting was an exchange of insults.[32]

Old World history is mostly a soap opera with guns. Remembering the details is like trying to keep track of friendships and rivalries on a soap opera and about as enlightening. I am giving you some of the details here only so that you can get a taste of Old World politics.

Napoleon III did not like the idea of having an enemy to his east and south. He was afraid of being attacked on two fronts. He complained.

Leopold backed off, declining the Spanish throne.

Napoleon III apparently thought the Prussians needed to be taught a lesson, however, so he declared war on them anyhow, starting the Franco-Prussian war.

Not a smart move. The French lost, and Napoleon III was taken prisoner. In Paris the French people rose up (again), overthrew their government (again), and declared a republic (again). The French have been big on revolutions.

The important point for us today is that the Prussians were not satisfied with the demise of the French monarchy. They demanded, and got, a formal surrender, plus France's northeast provinces of Alsace and Lorraine, and **reparations**.[33]

The French felt they were unfairly punished. Those who lose usually do, and therein lay the seeds of the next war, and the next, and so on.

Riding high from victory over the French, the popular Bismarck talked the Prussian states and their neighbors into a new alliance, a union into the country called Germany.

---

[32] Grolier Encyclopedia, article about Franco-Prussian War.

[33] Reparations: money, land or goods forced from a defeated nation as compensation for damage or injury during a war.

Important date: On January 18, 1871, the German Empire was proclaimed, with Wilhelm of Prussia as its emperor. Chris, notice that Wilhelm's title was Kaiser, which means Caesar, after the emperors of the old Roman Empire.

Uncle Eric

14

Ancient German Ambitions

Dear Chris,

Thanks to propaganda from World War II, especially the film series WHY WE FIGHT and its successor VICTORY AT SEA, many Americans believe that Germany has been a source of war and tyranny in Europe for centuries. Films, books, and articles sometimes refer to "ancient German ambitions."

There are no ancient German ambitions. Germany was not a country until 1871.

To explain away this uncomfortable fact, some propagandists say that Germany is just the modern name for Prussia, and the Prussians were obsessed with military power. Prussian ideas supposedly infected German officers during both World Wars.

There are two small problems with this reasoning.

First, Prussia originated more than a thousand years ago in what is today called Lithuania, far to the east of Germany, and, for most of its history, Prussia was centered in what is now called Poland. Prussia did not extend to the Rhine River until 1814.

Second, the very first attempt to kill Hitler was by his generals.

Strange behavior for a group of militarists dedicated to blindly obeying orders.

Many of Hitler's generals were Christian and believed in a Higher Law than any government's law.[34]

They new Hitler was evil and made several attempts to kill him, including the most famous, at Rastenburg, by Colonel Claus von Stauffenberg and his group. Hitler said he did not trust any of his generals, and when he thought of them they made him ill.[35]

So the "ancient German ambition" to conquer the world did not exist because it could not exist — there was no ancient Germany. And if German officers were infected with Prussian ideas that supposedly required blind obedience, why were they the first Germans to try to kill Hitler?

Some Germans had the desire for conquest, no doubt about it, but to say that Germans were or are more obsessed with war than the rest of Europe is nonsense, a form of bigotry.

If you check the CENTENNIA® program, you will find the French and Austro-Hungarians (Habsburgs) were into the sport of conquest many centuries before the Germans.

Leaders of Prussia did have a desire for conquest — try to find a European ruler who didn't — but the true heavyweight thugs of Europe were the French and Austro-Hungarians; they were the source of most of the worst warfare since the Middle Ages.

As you can see from my previous letter about the Franco-Prussian War, had it not been for the French attack on the Prussians in 1870, Germany may not even have been formed.

Uncle Eric

---

[34] HITLER'S GERMAN ENEMIES, by Louis L. Snyder, Hippocrene Books, NY, 1990.

[35] THE GERMAN GENERAL STAFF, by Walter Goerlitz, Frederick A. Praeger, Inc, NY, tenth printing in 1959, p.434.

15

Political Power

Dear Chris,

Previously I mentioned two deadly ideas that have driven many countries to war. One is the Pax Romana and the other is its offspring, fascism. Before we go further *we need to look at the third, and the most important, idea that helps cause wars: political power.*

What is political power?

The best way to answer is to ask two more questions.

How do you know a government is a government?

What makes this "public" organization different from businesses, churches, charities, and other "private" organizations?

Government is the institution that has the legal privilege of using force on persons who have not harmed anyone. This privilege is what sets it apart from all other institutions.

Generally, this privilege is felt most in the form of taxes. When a government collects a tax from you, it is saying, buy what we are selling or people with guns will come to your home and haul you away to prison.

No other institution can do this to you. For example, if you send a letter to an automobile company telling them you refuse to purchase their cars, what will happen?

Nothing. You might get a letter of apology saying, "We are sorry that you are not happy with our products, what can we do to win you back?" But there will be no threats.

What might happen to a person who, at income tax time, sends a similar letter to the Internal Revenue Service saying he does not like the services the government provides and refuses to pay for them.

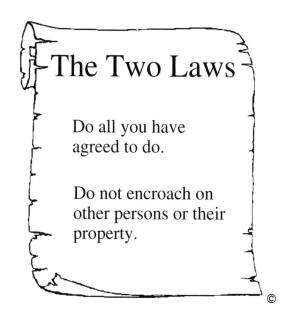

The Two Laws

Do all you have agreed to do.

Do not encroach on other persons or their property.

©

Will he get a letter of apology? Not likely. He will be told politely but firmly that if he doesn't buy what the government is selling he will be in deep trouble.

So political power is the legal privilege of using force on persons who have not harmed anyone. This power is what makes government different. Can you think of any situation in which government's decisions are not backed by force or threats of force?

If you do not like the services of a private organization, you can walk away. With government, you cannot walk away.

In my earlier letter I explained the two laws that make civilization possible.

The first: Do all you have agreed to do.

The second: Do not encroach on other persons or their property.

Political power is the legal privilege of violating these laws. This is why the American Founders were so afraid of government and tried to keep it severely limited.

Here are some thoughts about political power:

Government is not reason; it is not eloquence; it is force. Like fire, it is a dangerous servant and a fearful master.

— George Washington

Society in every state is a blessing, but government, even in its best state is but a necessary evil; in its worst state, an intolerable one.

— Thomas Paine

I am more and more convinced that man is a dangerous creature; and that power, whether vested in many or a few, is ever grasping, and, like the grave, cries "Give, give."

— Abigail Adams

An honest man can feel no pleasure in the exercise of power over his fellow citizens.

— Thomas Jefferson

Journalist H.L. Mencken once observed that, "The urge to save humanity is almost always a false-face for the urge to rule it."

This brings us to the important point for you and me at the moment: *the love of power is probably the main driving force behind wars.*

If you are a powerseeker, what would be the point of spending your whole life trying to acquire power if, once you got it, you could not use it on someone?

Powerseekers are always looking for someone they can make dance to their tune.

Sometimes they cannot easily use their power on persons in their own countries. Perhaps, as in the case of the United States, there is a Constitution and Bill of Rights that restrict their ability to coerce others. Or, maybe persons in their own country are heavily armed and able to defend themselves.

In such cases, powerseekers often look abroad for persons who are not well protected.

In other cases, the pain they can inflict at home is not enough to satisfy them — the names Stalin and Hitler come to mind — and they go looking abroad for more people to hurt.

If a person wants political power, this is a strong indication he cannot be trusted with it. This is why the American Founders wanted the Federal Government to be kept small and weak. Jefferson said, "In questions of power...let no more be heard of confidence in man, but bind him down from mischief by the chains of the Constitution."

But today in every country people are trusted with power, and they all too often have free reign to use it; the result is war.

The use of military force is the most extreme form of political power and so the most satisfying.

Chris, try to imagine, if you were the kind of person who enjoyed making up laws to force others to bend to your will, what would it be like to unleash battleships, tanks, and bombers on them? Imagine the thrill.

So far, I have identified three deadly ideas — the Pax Romana, fascism, and political power. You also know something about the behavior of European rulers leading up to the World Wars. Now let's return to America for a while and look at the behavior of the USG. This behavior was not much better than that of the Europeans.

Are you beginning to see now why I say that in the case of World War I, the events *in* the war are not as important as the ideas and events leading *to* the war?

If not, Chris, I think you soon will.

Uncle Eric

16

Global Protection

Dear Chris,

In 1975, the crew of the American merchant ship *Mayaguez* knowingly sailed into pirate-infested waters near war-torn Cambodia. Khmer Rouge pirates captured them.

President Ford sent navy ships and marines to rescue the ship and its crew. In the battle with the pirates, the 40 crewmen were saved, but 42 marines and sailors were killed and 50 were wounded.

This brings us to the fourth deadly idea that gets us into wars: ***global protection****.* The belief in global protection has disappeared almost everywhere except in America. Americans may be the only people on earth who still believe they have a right to go anywhere outside their home country and if they get into trouble, call on soldiers, sailors, and airmen to risk their lives rescuing them.

Global protection was once an attitude held by the British, and perhaps the French, Italians, and a few others. Today these others all know that when they go abroad they go at their own risk, and if they do not like the risk they should not go. Americans are the only exception. I do not know why.

We do know that the idea of global protection for Americans sprang up during the Barbary Wars, which were fought just after the U.S. Government was founded.

In those days, American merchant ships were sailing through Atlantic and Mediterranean waters that had belonged to Islamic powers for centuries. The Muslims were levying a tax on them. Sometimes when Americans refused to pay the tax, the ships and crews were captured. The owners of the ships asked the new U.S. Government for help, and the USG sent the Navy to fight the Muslims. The Muslims were called pirates.

As I write this today, Muslims who are still fighting the USG are called terrorists. As you recall, I explained all this to you in my previous set of letters about THE THOUSAND YEAR WAR IN THE MIDEAST.[36]

The Barbary Wars set the precedent for the U.S. Government to send the armed forces to rescue people who have gone abroad and gotten into trouble.

In other words, the Barbary Wars set the precedent for risking the lives of soldiers, sailors, and airmen to bail out people who gambled and lost.

Once the precedent was set, powerseekers were quick to use the armed forces whenever the opportunity arose. I count no less than 52 cases during the 1800s of the Marines being sent abroad in actions that had nothing to do with defending our homeland.

During the 20th century, U.S. forces were sent abroad into harm's way no less than 188 times.[37]

Chris, how do you feel about that? The day is not far away when you will be old enough to march off to war. Have you given any thought to what you are willing to die for?

Uncle Eric

---

[36] Uncle Eric is referring to the book THE THOUSAND YEAR WAR IN THE MIDEAST: HOW IT AFFECTS YOU TODAY by Richard J. Maybury, published by Bluestocking Press, web site: www.BluestockingPress.com

[37] U.S. Navy official web site, and "Presidents Have A History...," by L. Gordon Crovitz, WALL STREET JOURNAL, January 15, 1987, p.24.

17

Interests

Dear Chris,

The fifth deadly idea that gets America into wars is:
"interests." Military personnel are sent around the globe to
die defending America's "interests," but no one knows what
an interest is. The word is not defined in the Constitution or
in law. All we can be sure about is that the USG assumes
that soldiers, sailors, and airmen have an obligation to die
for interests.

In December 1998, for instance, President Clinton ordered
the bombing of Iraq. He said it was "to protect the national
interests of the United States."[38]

A month before, the WALL STREET JOURNAL ran an editorial
by former Assistant Undersecretary of Defense Zalmay
Khalilzad, saying that Iraq was an "obstacle to U.S. regional
interests."[39]

On January 22, 1997, Defense Secretary Cohen told the
Senate Armed Services Committee that "military forces
should only be used if they advance U.S. interests."[40] He
did not say what an interest is, or why it is worth dying for.

In 1994, former U.S. Ambassador Roger Harrison
complained that "every half-baked general and warlord in
the world feels free to ignore our interests."[41] Again, he did
not define interests.

---

[38] SACRAMENTO BEE newspaper, December 17, 1998, p.1.

[39] WALL STREET JOURNAL, "A Turning Point..", Nov. 13, 1998, p.18.

[40] ARMY TIMES, February 3, 1997, p.13.

[41] U.S. NEWS & WORLD REPORT, July 25, 1994, p.22.

The Clinton administration even issued the decree that "U.S. national security interests are at stake in Georgia."[42] They were talking not about the state of Georgia in the United States, but about the tiny country of Georgia in the former U.S.S.R.

Chris, do you even know where Georgia is? Look at a globe. It's just north of Armenia and west of Azerbaijan, on the Black Sea, south of Russia.

Is there something in Georgia that *you* would be willing to die for?

This is a pattern that goes back two centuries to the Barbary Wars. Interests have never been defined, but members of the armed forces have been ordered to fight and die for them.

My guess as to why interests have not been defined is that nearly all the cases are similar to that of the *Mayaguez.* Someone went abroad to invest money, or maybe just to visit as a tourist, then got into trouble and expected to be rescued. They gambled and lost, then demanded that young soldiers, sailors, and airmen risk their lives to bail them out.

This use of the armed forces, not for defense of the homeland, but for a global rescue service to protect "interests," has made Americans more willing to take travel risks and quicker to do business in strange, far off lands.

In other words, it has made them more willing to gamble.

One of these far off lands was Japan. An island nation, Japan has no borders with other nations. In the 1800s, the Japanese remained secluded from the outside world, refusing to do business with anyone except the Chinese and Dutch.

---

[42] RESOURCE WARS, by Michael T. Klare, Metropolitan Books, NY. 2001, p.95.

American companies wanted to conduct business there, and they persuaded President Millard Fillmore to do something about it.

Japan was on the other side of the Pacific and no conceivable threat, but Commodore Matthew Perry was sent to intimidate the Japanese by sailing his warships into Tokyo Bay.

On March 31, 1854, the frightened Japanese emperor signed a treaty that allowed U.S. merchants to do business in two Japanese cities. The treaty also enabled U.S. ships to buy coal in Japan, thus giving the Navy the ability to operate in the Orient, far from America.

This is called **gunboat diplomacy**. It means using military forces to frighten foreigners into signing agreements.

So, by 1855, the U.S. Government's practice of gunboat diplomacy to protect "interests" was fully in effect, and the idea that the armed forces were strictly for defense of our homeland was gone.

Uncle Eric

P.S. Chris, sometimes Americans are told they must send their sons and daughters to war to protect our access to oil sold by other nations. This oil is regarded as a "vital interest" and is, therefore, thought to be worth American lives.

Rarely does anyone ask the question, how much blood are you willing to pay for a barrel of oil, and are you willing to pay with your own blood or only with the blood of others?

Besides, if a regime that hates the West captures an oil field, what are they going to do with the oil, drink it?

They can get little benefit from it unless they sell it.

They might somehow charge a higher price, but the question then becomes, are you willing to die to keep the price of gasoline down?

18

Cost Externalization

Dear Chris,

Recently I met an American woman who had gone on a safari to Africa. While in the wilderness, her group was attacked by bandits. The woman said she was appalled. As the bullets were whizzing around her, she kept expecting the Marines to appear and whisk her to safety. The Marines did not appear, of course, and several Americans were killed. She was outraged.

For persons inside their homeland, the police and military forces are pledged to protect them to the fullest extent possible. History is replete with examples of troops and police giving their lives to protect the innocent.

Outside the homeland is a different matter. All governments, including the USG, have the same *spoken* policy for persons who want to visit or do business in foreign lands: when an individual or firm goes abroad, they go at their own risk, and if they do not like the risk they should not go.

However, actions speak louder than words, and, in its actions, the USG has undermined this policy. It endlessly sends its armed forces to rescue Americans in other lands. This creates a false sense of security for travelers who are naive about real politics, like the woman I mentioned above.

Another example is the rescue mission to Sierra Leone in 1997. Hundreds of Americans were visiting Sierra Leone despite its five-year civil war. In May, the fighting became so intense that some of the Americans were in danger of being caught in the crossfire.

The amphibious assault ship *Kearsarge* was sent, and U.S. Marine and Army troops were ordered to risk their lives pulling the Americans out of danger.

It is these kinds of rescues that give American tourists and business people the impression they have the right to be protected by the armed forces no matter where they go. American businesses have invested billions of dollars in other countries, building factories, offices, and plantations on the assumption that if things turn ugly, they will be bailed out.

Sometimes they are, and sometimes not. The Marines spent decades in Latin America trying to protect the United Fruit Company and its banana plantations. But in 2001, when Exxon-Mobil's natural gas facilities in Indonesia were attacked, Exxon-Mobil was not bailed out.

During the Middle Ages, people had a much more realistic attitude about protection. Along the Dordogne River in France you can see ancient fortified mills. In those days, business people knew that if they set up a mill in a high-risk area, they had to provide for its protection. They erected stone walls, moats, and other fortifications bristling with cannon.

If the threats were so severe that the cost of fortifications would be prohibitively expensive, the mills were not built and workers were not sent there.

In other words, the cost of fortifications was a control on risk. If threats were so great that the necessary fortifications would be highly expensive, the risks would not be taken.

Ships at sea were equipped the same way. Merchants' vessels carried cannons, muskets, and swords, and crews were trained to use them. They knew that the Navy could not suddenly appear as if by magic to rescue them. Ship owners and captains avoided waters that were so high risk that their weapons might not be sufficient, or they had to pay their crews extra to take the higher risks.

Today, American tourists and business people are allowed to do what economists call **cost externalization.** Cost externalization means shifting a risk or expense onto someone else.

When soldiers, sailors, and airmen, as in the case of Sierra Leone, rescue American tourists and business people in other lands, the cost of taking the risk is shifted onto the soldiers, sailors, and airmen, and onto the taxpayers who are paying the expenses.

When the cost externalization does not occur, as in the case of the naive woman on the safari, people often die.

This American tradition of externalizing the cost of going abroad is a major reason America gets into wars, including the two World Wars. Americans send their ships, their money, or themselves abroad, then when they become trapped in a war, they call on the armed forces to help. The armed forces, and the whole country, are then in the war. *Cost externalization is the sixth deadly idea that leads to war.*

In future letters I will give you examples of cost externalization getting us into wars. One was the case of the sinking of the passenger liner *Lusitania* in World War I. Another was the sinking of the destroyer *Rueben James* in World War II. In both cases, the USG was sending war supplies to the government of Britain, and the government of Germany found out about it and started shooting. In effect, the USG allowed the government of Britain to externalize its costs of fighting Germans onto Americans; the Americans paid with their lives.

Uncle Eric

19

Manifest Destiny

Dear Chris,

Now that you understand a few more of the deadly *ideas* that lead to war, let's look at more of the *events* leading to the World Wars.

By the mid-1800s, the Industrial Revolution, which began in England, had given powerseekers in Europe amazing new weapons that were available in few other countries. While much of the earth's population was still using bows and arrows, the Europeans were building battleships.

Never before or since has there been such an opportunity for powerseekers. Europeans conquered almost the entire world. We do not know how many people they killed, but it was certainly many millions.

At the Battle of the Pyramids in Egypt, Napoleon's troops had muskets and cannons. The **Mamelukes**[43] had swords. Napoleon lost 30 men; the Mamelukes lost 5,000.

Each conquest gave the Europeans more land and more taxpayers.

Powerseekers in Washington D.C. were jealous; they, too, wanted a global empire.

---

[43] Mamelukes: a military group originally composed of slaves from Turkey. They ruled Egypt from about 1250 until 1517, and remained powerful there until 1811.

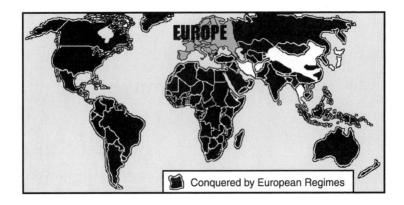

Conquered by European Regimes

Europe is only 6.6% of the earth's land surface, but Europeans inherited the Roman lust for one world government. The first to acquire advanced weapons produced by the Industrial Revolution, Europeans attacked and conquered all the rest of the globe, with only five exceptions. Persia (Iran), Afghanistan, Thailand, Japan, and most of China were able to beat them off, but only Japan escaped terrible death and destruction.

In 1845 a New York editor, John L. O'Sullivan, had written that it was "the fulfillment of our manifest destiny to overspread the continent allotted by Providence for the free development of our yearly expanding millions."

In other words, Sullivan said God had given the U.S. Government the right to capture and rule all the land from the Atlantic to the Pacific regardless of who might already be living there.

The Conqueror

The Industrial Revolution began in England, so the first continent to gain industrialization was Europe.

At a time when much of the world was still armed with bows and arrows, the Europeans were building battleships, such as the 22,600-ton Orion class "Conqueror" below.

London began construction of its Orion class ships in 1909. The armor was a foot thick. The ships could travel more than 20 mph, and their ten large cannons could fire 13.5-inch diameter shells more than five miles.

This is why Europeans were able to conquer most of the world. What could a bow and arrow do against a battleship?

This situation has ended. Industrialization has spread to every corner of the globe, so even the least developed nations have access to modern weapons. In the 1980s, primitive tribesmen in Afghanistan were able to acquire shoulder-launched guided missiles and defeat the USSR, the second most powerful nation in history.

However, the descendants of the millions conquered by the Europeans have little good to say about Europe, and Washington's alliances with European governments do not do America's reputation any good.

This was music to the ears of powerseekers, and they lost no time making their **Manifest Destiny**[44] a reality. *Manifest Destiny is the seventh deadly idea that leads to war.*

The Civil War caused a delay, but by 1890, nearly all the land from coast to coast had been taken, and powerseekers were looking for new realms to conquer. The drive for a global empire was under way.

One problem. The Europeans had already conquered most of the world, carving it up like a Thanksgiving turkey for their own personal use. In order for the USG to have a global empire, they would need to take land and taxpayers away from the Europeans.

Work on this project began in 1884 with establishment of the Naval War College at Newport, Rhode Island.

During the Civil War, the Union Navy had 700 ships, but most were scrapped after the war. By 1880, only 48 obsolete warships remained because America experienced no military threat.

America was the undisputed industrial giant of the world capable of producing unimaginable amounts of highly advanced weapons. In addition, it had two giant moats protecting it — the Atlantic and Pacific oceans — plus a large, armed population willing to fight to defend it. In no capital on earth would an attack on America be seriously considered. Hence, voters had no desire to spend money on a navy.

The lack of a navy was frustrating to **imperialists.**[45] The airplane had not yet been invented, so without ships, these

---

[44] Manifest Destiny: the belief that God gave the U.S. Government the right to capture and rule all the land from the Atlantic to the Pacific.

[45] Imperialist: one who wishes to conquer others and force them into his empire.

people had no easy way to "project power" (the modern Pentagon term) into other lands.

In 1890, the president of the Naval War College, Alfred Thayer Mahan, published his three-volume work, THE INFLUENCE OF SEA POWER ON HISTORY. Arguing for a strong navy, Mahan quickly became the high priest of America's growing imperialist movement. Construction of a new fleet of warships began.

The next question was, which of the European powers was weak enough to be easily beaten? The answer will be given in my next letter. It is a highly important step to World War I.

Uncle Eric

20

The Splendid Little War

Dear Chris,

In my last letter, I left you with the question, "Which of the European powers was weak enough to be easily beaten?"

The answer was Spain. For almost four centuries, Spain had owned a huge empire in the Western Hemisphere, stretching from California to the southern tip of South America.

By the 1890s, Spanish military power was old and feeble, and the empire was falling apart. Part of this empire was Cuba.

For thirty years, Cubans had been in rebellion against Spanish rule. The warfare was a danger to U.S. "interests," meaning the plantations and other businesses in which Americans had invested in Cuba. The war was also a threat to Americans who chose to spend their vacations on the island.

To protect these risk-takers, President William McKinley sent the battleship *Maine* into Havana's harbor.

The *Maine* exploded, killing 260 crew members.[46]

Earlier, Theodore Roosevelt, who was Assistant Secretary of the Navy and a leader of the imperialist movement, said, "I should welcome almost any war, for I think this country needs one. If we lose our virile, manly qualities, and sink

---

[46] Grolier Encyclopedia CD, under "*Maine,* the ship."

into a nation of mere hucksters, then we shall indeed reach a condition worse than that of the ancient civilizations in the years of their decay."[47]

The destruction of the *Maine* gave the imperialists the war they were hoping for. Spain was blamed for the explosion, and on April 11, 1898, President McKinley delivered a war message to Congress saying, "The naval court of inquiry, which, it is needless to say, commands the unqualified confidence of the government, was unanimous in its conclusion that the destruction of the *Maine* was caused by an exterior explosion — that of a submarine mine."

Congress declared war on Spain. The only significant opposition was from the business and financial community. Most had no "interests" in Cuba and were afraid the war would wreck the U.S. economy.[48] But they were shouted down.

Under the battle cry "Remember the *Maine!*" America's armed forces were ordered to attack the Spanish in Cuba — and in the Philippines. It is not quite clear what the Philippines, on the other side of the world, had to do with protecting Americans in Cuba, but this "minor technicality" was ignored, and U.S. forces were sent to the Philippines.

War fever was so intense that when McKinley called for 200,000 volunteers, he got more than a million.

The entire male student body of Lafayette College in Pennsylvania volunteered.[49]

---

[47] "CRUCIBLE OF EMPIRE — THE SPANISH-AMERICAN WAR," PBS documentary.

[48] A HISTORY OF THE UNITED STATES by Williams, Current & Freidel, Alfred A. Knopf Publisher, New York, 1965, p.257.

[49] "CRUCIBLE OF EMPIRE — THE SPANISH-AMERICAN WAR," PBS documentary.

In the Philippines, Admiral Dewey sailed into Manila Bay. His nine modern warships attacked Spain's sixteen outdated ships.

It was a massacre. Shouting, "Remember the *Maine!*" Americans destroyed ten Spanish ships at a cost of one American life, a sailor who died of heat stroke.

The story was similar in Cuba. The modern American equipment made short work of the Spanish army and navy.

The Spanish surrendered, and the U.S. ambassador to England, John Milton, called it a "splendid little war."

At the Treaty of Paris on December 10, 1898, neither the Cubans nor the Filipinos were allowed to take part in the negotiations about their futures. Their homelands were simply annexed by the USG as the first parts of the new U.S. Empire.

Incidentally, Chris, the idea of Manifest Destiny is not dead, it just isn't called that anymore. As I write this letter, a single new name has not yet emerged, but during the late 1990s, Secretary of State Madeleine Albright tried to give it one. The WASHINGTON POST ran a story about "Albright's frequent, triumphal references to the supremacy of U.S. power and values — to America as 'the indispensable nation.'"[50]

In 1998, Albright announced, "If we have to use force, it is because we are America. We are the indispensable nation. We stand tall. We see farther into the future."[51]

---

[50] "No Clout Where It Counts," by John Lancaster, WASHINGTON POST NATIONAL WEEKEND EDITION, April 17, 2000

[51] BLOWBACK, by Chalmers Johnson, Henry Holt and Company, NY, 2000, p.217.

I am reminded of the warning, "Pride goeth before destruction, and a haughty spirit before a fall." No truer words were ever written.

Under the doctrine of Indispensable Nation, the widely held belief in Washington D.C. is that Americans have the right and duty to intervene in other nations.

This should remind us of H.L. Mencken's remark, "The urge to save humanity is almost always a false-face for the urge to rule it."

Few Americans see it this way, but we can safely bet that millions in other countries do, and many of them have guns and bombs.

Chris, whenever you think about the destruction of the World Trade Center, or the war that grew out of it, remember Albright and the doctrine of Indispensable Nation, or Manifest Destiny — the seventh deadly idea that leads to war.

Uncle Eric

21

Guerrilla War

Dear Chris,

To reiterate, the ideas and events that led to World War I are much more important than events during the war. This is why it is essential for you to understand the Spanish-American War and other events between that war and World War I.

However, before we get further into those events, you need to know something about military strategy and tactics, so we will divert to that for a while.

In this and several of my next letters, I will review a concept that I discussed in my previous set of letters to you on THE THOUSAND YEAR WAR IN THE MIDEAST.[52] At that time, I introduced you to a concept few Americans understand, guerrilla war. This is even more important today than it was during the Spanish-American War or during the World Wars. Most wars today are guerrilla wars, including the one that began with the destruction of the World Trade Center.

When historians examine wars, they rarely look at the people who found ways to stay out of them. To me this is

---

[52] Uncle Eric is referring to Chapter 15, "The Invincible Secret Weapon" in the book THE THOUSAND YEAR WAR IN THE MIDEAST: HOW IT AFFECTS YOU TODAY by Richard J. Maybury, published by Bluestocking Press, web site: www.BluestockingPress.com

strange. I think one of the most important lessons that history should teach is how to stay out of wars. What skill could be more valuable?

So we will look at the nation that has the best track record at staying out of wars, Switzerland.

The Swiss have always had the deck stacked against them. They live right in the heart of Europe, which means right in the heart of the most violent, bloody part of the earth. But, at the time I write this letter, they have not been in a foreign war in two centuries; the Swiss even stayed out of both World Wars despite being entirely surrounded by these wars.

In my opinion, Chris, every parent who cares about his or her children should be clamoring for the USG to switch to what I will call the "Swiss system of defense."

So how have the Swiss stayed out of wars?

You need to understand guerrilla war. Here is the story.

According to the AMERICAN HERITAGE DICTIONARY, a guerrilla is "a member of an irregular, usually indigenous military or paramilitary unit operating in small bands in occupied territory to harass and undermine the enemy, as by surprise raids."

Guerrillas are not uniformed "regular" troops, they are militia — so-called citizen-soldiers like those required by the Second Amendment to the U.S. Constitution.

Regulars are sometimes called conventional troops; they are what Americans think of when they think of soldiers.

A guerrilla is a farmer, merchant, or taxi driver by day, and a sniper or saboteur by night. His style is hit-and-run.

A key point is that a guerrilla usually will not attack unless he is sure he can escape cleanly.

In the Mel Gibson movie THE PATRIOT, Gibson's character is based on the "Swamp Fox," Francis Marion, from the American Revolutionary War. Marion was one of the most successful guerrillas in history. His troops rarely numbered more than 200 and often just a few dozen, but, using guerrilla tactics, this handful of part-time warriors kept thousands of the enemy tied down. They prevented the successful **occupation** of the whole state of South Carolina.

The main problem regular troops have in fighting guerrillas is that they cannot shoot what they cannot find. How do you tell the difference between people who are just ordinary farmers, merchants, and taxi drivers, and those who are secretly planting booby traps and sniping at you?

Because a single guerrilla can keep a whole **battalion** [53] tied up for weeks, the rule of thumb among military experts is that conventional troops need at least a six-to-one numerical superiority over guerrillas. If guerrillas number 1,000, the regulars fighting them will need to number at least 6,000.

This is an optimistic estimate. In 1998, the Turkish government had 200,000 conventional troops committed to fighting just 1,200 Kurdish guerrillas. This was a ratio of 166 to one. You cannot shoot what you cannot find.

In an interview on January 1, 1959, Cuban dictator Fulgencio Batista said, "A government needs one hundred soldiers for every guerrilla it faces."[54] A few days later

---

[53] Battalion: in the infantry, about 800 troops. Typically, but not always, there are nine troops in a squad, three squads to a platoon, four platoons to a company, six companies to a battalion, two battalions to a brigade, and six brigades to a division.

[54] POWER QUOTES, by Daniel B. Baker, Visible Ink Press, Detroit, MI, 1992, p.337.

Batista's troops were beaten by the guerrillas. Batista fled and was replaced by Fidel Castro.

This is why the Second Amendment is in the Constitution. When a militia is well-armed and trained to fight an invader by using guerrilla tactics, as the American militia was during the Revolution — and the Swiss militia has been for hundreds of years — an invader needs a force so large that no one is likely to try it.

In my next letter, Chris, I will tell you more about guerrilla warfare.

Uncle Eric

22

Guerrilla War Examples

Dear Chris,

Switzerland stayed out of the World Wars; yet Switzerland is smaller than Ohio in both population and area. How did the Swiss do it?

Their story is very enlightening, but not usually revealed in school textbooks. Consequently, many people today are unaware that Switzerland has a crucially important lesson to teach.

In Switzerland, a man joins the militia at age 20 and remains until age 50 (officers remain until age 55). A militia is all the able-bodied adult males of good character[55] in the country. They are trained, equipped, and ready at all times to turn out for guerrilla operations.

Contrary to the unflattering picture of militias often painted by the news media, a militia is a military version of the volunteer firemen who are always trained and ready to turn out to fight fires.

Each Swiss militiaman trains regularly, much like the National Guard in the U.S. He keeps his battle rifle and ammunition in his home ready for immediate use.

Militia-guerrillas are trained to ambush privates and corporals only when a more valuable target is not available. They prefer colonels and generals.

---

[55] In this context, good character usually means no criminal record.

Switzerland in the World Wars

■ **In war** □ **Not in war**

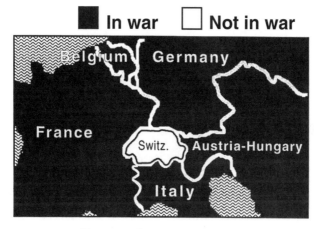

Europe in World War I

Europe in World War II

Despite living in the exact center of the most bloodsoaked part of the world — Europe — the Swiss have not been in a foreign war in almost two centuries. Yet, few historians or military analysts bother to ask, how do the Swiss do it?

Marksmanship is the Swiss national sport, and all Swiss militiamen are required to be expert marksmen. This means they are all qualified to be snipers, and the colonels and generals of surrounding nations know it.

There is an old saying, Switzerland does not have an army; Switzerland *is* an army. It is an entire nation of Minutemen.

In World War II, the Swiss militia numbered 850,000, a fifth of the population. These were more troops than the U.S. Army had when the World Trade Center was destroyed. Not bad for such a small country.

Under the six-to-one ratio, the Germans and Italians would have needed five million troops to successfully occupy that tiny nation. Facing 850,000 snipers, the German generals decided they could invade, but they would never get out of Switzerland alive.

Thousands of Swiss women also acquired rifles and practiced their marksmanship. As I write this today, on any weekend, you can go to a rifle range in Switzerland and see women practicing to earn their sharpshooting medals.

The Swiss also had aircraft and other heavy weapons, but the backbone of the defense was the militiaman, the sniper who was always fully trained and ready to hunt down the enemy's leaders.

Any European nation could have used the militia-guerrilla system, and a few did make a halfhearted attempt, but none came close to doing it as well as the Swiss, so the other countries were easier targets.

Chris, Switzerland has long been famous for the effectiveness of its militia and for its heavily armed neutrality. If you will read FEDERALIST PAPERS number 20, 42, and 43 by James Madison and Alexander Hamilton, you will find that in creating the American system, the Founders studied Switzerland. The Second Amendment and Tenth Amendment to the Constitution especially bear the imprint of Swiss thinking.

Nothing strikes terror into the heart of a general like the prospect of invading a country infested with snipers.

This is not to say the Swiss are perfect. They are human and they make mistakes.

As I said earlier, Chris, at the time I write this letter, neutral Switzerland has not been in a war in two centuries. When other nations gave a war and sent out the invitations, the Swiss sent back a polite but firm, no thank you.

However, pressure on the Swiss to abandon their neutrality has been growing for decades. In February 2002, the Swiss caved in and voted to join the United Nations. At the time I write this letter, the Vatican is the only nation voluntarily outside the UN. The Swiss model of heavily armed neutrality is fading away. I suggest you study it to learn all you can, before it is gone.

I'll try to answer the question I anticipate you might ask in your next letter: why don't all countries use this system? My guess: a militia-guerrilla force cannot be used to invade other people's homelands. Militiamen are only part-time soldiers. Because they have civilian jobs and families to take care of, a militia is strictly defensive, not offensive.

Also, most governments have so much power that their subjects (their citizens) hate them, and I am sure these rulers do not want their subjects to have weapons.

Today, if we used the militia-guerrilla system of defense required by the Second Amendment, the U.S. could field 50 million able-bodied males. This means an invader would need, at a minimum, 300 million troops.

All the armed forces of the rest of the world combined total less than 40 million.[56]

Try to imagine invading a country infested with 50 million snipers.

Incidentally, Chris, let me point out the exact wording of the Second Amendment:

> A well regulated militia, being necessary to the security of a free State, the right of the people to keep and bear arms, shall not be infringed.

The right "to keep and bear arms" clause gets most of the press, but notice that the militia clause comes first.

Also, notice that the militia clause does not say, "A well regulated militia, being optional for the security of a free State." It says "necessary."

In other words, the amendment does not give *permission* for a well-regulated militia; it *requires* one. The American Founders were no fools.

After all, it was the Pennsylvania flintlock rifle (invented by immigrant gunsmiths from Germany, incidentally) used as a sniper rifle that enabled Minutemen to keep the Redcoats from controlling America. British officers had a terrible fear of that rifle. Sniper Timothy Murphy is credited with winning the battle of Saratoga by killing both British commanders. With their leaders dead, the battle turned against the British.[57]

The psychological effects of a militia are even more powerful than mere numbers would suggest. We get a hint

---

[56] THE STATE OF WAR AND PEACE ATLAS by Dan Smith, Penguin Reference, London, 1997, p.64.

[57] "The Ten Most Important Guns in History," TALES OF THE GUN, History Channel Documentary.

of one effect from the Swiss sniper incident in World War II. It grew out of the legend of William Tell.

Chris, in case you have not heard the legend of William Tell, it takes place in 1307.

Here's how the story goes.

Switzerland has been invaded and conquered by the Austrians, and the Swiss are in revolt against Austrian rule.

The Swiss are fanatics about liberty (every bit as much as Americans).

Having trouble putting down the Swiss rebellion, the Austrians try to make examples of Swiss rebels who are caught.

In a Swiss village, the Austrians place an Austrian hat on a pole and command all the Swiss to salute it whenever they pass by, as if it is an Austrian army officer.

Tell is walking through the village one day and refuses to salute. As punishment, an Austrian official orders him to shoot an apple off his son's head.

If Tell is a bad shot, his son will die.

Chris, the only conclusion to this story that most Americans know is that Tell proves to be a good shot. He hits the apple without harming his son. But there's more to the legend.

> After Tell hits the apple without harming his son, an arrow falls from Tell's shirt, and Tell says to the Austrian official, if my son had been harmed, this arrow would have been for you.

Here's the rest of the story that few American's know, but the Swiss take very seriously.

> Tell is a guerrilla who plans to kill the emperor, and after the apple incident, his plan is discovered; he is captured and thrown aboard a ship as a prisoner.
>
> However, Tell escapes, then hunts down the official who made him shoot the apple off his son's head, and kills him.
>
> Tell then leads a general uprising in which the emperor is killed, and the Austrians withdraw, leaving Switzerland a free country.

As I write this letter, Switzerland remains one of the freest countries in the world.

No one knows how much of the William Tell story is true, but, as I said, the Swiss take it very seriously.

The point to them is that the military objective is not to kill the enemy's troops. It is to kill enemy leaders.

Every Swiss grows up with this lesson drilled into his or her head. It is the reason for the Swiss emphasis on marksmanship. The Swiss tradition is to be a guerrilla marksman who goes after the highest ranking officers he can find.

This is a good generalization about all guerrillas. They prefer to go after colonels and generals or someone higher — not privates or corporals.

In 1938, a Swiss marksman named Maurice Bavaud sneaked into Germany. A theology student, Bavaud knew that Hitler's plans violated all ethical laws, especially the one that says, do not encroach on other persons or their property.

Bavaud stalked Hitler and fired at him on three separate occasions that we know of.

It is highly unlikely that a Swiss soldier would miss three times. All Swiss militiamen are required to be marksmen so that they can act as snipers if needed, and they are always equipped with superb rifles. It may be that, since the war had not yet begun, Bavaud was firing warning shots.

In any case, we can safely assume that the near misses made Hitler wonder how many more Swiss marksmen might be stalking him.

In 1941, Bavaud was caught and executed. Hitler personally forbade the play WILLIAM TELL from being performed or read in German schools, and he never tried to invade Switzerland.[58]

Note that Bavaud managed to stay hidden for three years. Were other Swiss snipers, hiding in Germany and Italy, pledged to kill the leaders if Switzerland was invaded?

---

[58] TARGET SWITZERLAND by Stephen P. Halbrook, Sarpedon Publishing, Rockville Center, NY, 1998, p.58 & 159.

We will probably never know. But if you were Hitler or Mussolini, what would you have thought?

The one thing we can be sure about is that in both World Wars tiny Switzerland was surrounded by warring powers but was not invaded. They had the deck stacked against them more completely than any other nation in history, but they stayed out of the war.

Incidentally, Chris, besides being the most heavily armed population in the world, the Swiss also have one of the lowest crime rates. In a country where a well-trained soldier with a battle rifle resides in almost every home, criminals know that their careers will likely be short and painful.

Firearm deaths are rare, too. These people take guns seriously. The whole country is trained in their safe and proper use.

Summarizing the Swiss experience in World War II, the Swiss essentially delivered a message to Axis rulers, the same one they had been delivering to foreign rulers for centuries: yes, you can probably beat us eventually, but by that time we will have hunted down and killed your officers, your henchmen, and you.

Axis rulers left the Swiss porcupine alone. So did the Russians and the other Allies.

And so did the Allies and the Central Powers in World War I.

One small insight: If you were Hitler and you were surrounded by officers who knew they would die if you attacked Switzerland, how much would you trust these officers?

How could you plan an invasion knowing that one of the officers might kill you if you so much as mentioned the idea of invading Switzerland?

Chris, if you will look at a map of every European war during the 19th and 20th centuries — the CENTENNIA® program is a good way to do this — you will find that in each case, in the center of all the bloodshed, is a little island of peace and freedom, Switzerland. The Swiss have had a few internal struggles, but foreign powers have left them alone.

Switzerland is not only a country, it is a citadel. Every village and every mountain pass is fortified. Every new house is built with a bomb shelter in the basement. The long, straight stretches of the expressways have been designed to do double-duty as military airstrips. The highway tunnels are bombproof hangars. Mountain caves are packed with enough food and ammunition for the whole population to conduct guerrilla operations for years.

To a tyrant, there is no place in the world as scary as Switzerland.

America has never had anything remotely resembling the Swiss system of protection. The American armed forces are not defensive, they are offensive. They are designed not to defend our homeland, but to get into other people's wars, and they do this very well. As I said in an earlier letter, during the 20th century, U.S. forces were sent abroad into other people's battles no less than 188 times.[59]

Nearly every book and movie about the World Wars omits Switzerland. The attitude of the writers seems to be, the Swiss were not in the wars, so they are not important; they are not part of the story.

To me, no country in the World Wars is more important than Switzerland. It is the example the others should be copying.

---

[59] U.S. Navy official web site, and "Presidents Have A History...," by L. Gordon Crovitz, WALL STREET JOURNAL, January 15, 1987, p.24.

Chris, who do you think I would say was the most significant person in the World Wars? I would say Maurice Bavaud. He showed how to stay out of the wars and how to stay free. What lesson could be more important?

A superb book about how the Swiss militia held the mighty German and Italian armies at bay in World War II is TARGET SWITZERLAND by Stephen P. Halbrook. I recommend this book highly. It will give you a far deeper understanding of the World Wars. In fact, all wars. It is one of the few cases of anyone asking, how did the Swiss do it?

Always remember, little Switzerland occupied the most dangerous location in the world — the exact center of Europe — entirely surrounded by enemies, but stayed out of both World Wars and stayed free.

The Swiss avoided the carnage so common all over the globe by doing what America's Second Amendment requires. They know a well-regulated militia is not optional, it is *necessary*. When it comes to achieving the peace and liberty we all want, I challenge you to find a system of military defense that has worked better than that of the Swiss. All countries can use it. I urge you again to study it while it is still there.

Chris, earlier I said it would be fair to say these are anti-war letters written by an extreme militarist. I hope you now understand what I mean.

Uncle Eric

P.S. In case you are wondering, Chris, as I write this, U.S. law prohibits the killing of foreign rulers. No one seems to be sure why this prohibition exists, but a common theory is that it is a way of protecting the U.S. President — it helps prevent tit-for-tat assassinations.

23

Never Surrender

Dear Chris,

Perhaps the most important characteristic of guerrillas is that they are independent. They have no commander-in-chief, no central leader; they almost always operate on their own personal initiative.

This gives the attacker no central authority on which he can focus his forces. It does him no good to capture the capitol and force the government to surrender. The guerrillas will fight on.

The invader must conquer his victims, city by city, town by town, village by village, and house by house. And, all the while, the country will be infested with snipers trying to shoot his officers.

If each house contains a well-trained, well-armed member of the militia who has taken an oath to never surrender, then the enemy is likely to run out of officers long before the militia runs out of snipers.

The reason the Afghans were able to beat the mighty Soviet army during the 1980s was because they had no government, and each guerrilla had sworn never to surrender.

In other words, a central authority is a convenience to the enemy; it gives him the ability to force surrender onto the whole country — just by conquering the government.

In World War II, Swiss militiamen took an oath never to surrender no matter what their government might be forced to say or do.[60] Chris, criminals and powerseekers consider peaceful Switzerland, where the whole population is armed against them, a bad example. The Swiss are often victims of smear campaigns. When you hear a condemnation of the Swiss, or any other group, do not form an opinion until you have all the facts; learn both sides of the story.

Uncle Eric

[60] TARGET SWITZERLAND by Stephen P. Halbrook, Sarpedon Publishing, Rockville Center, NY, 1998, p.58 & 172.

24

Killing Women

Dear Chris,

Before leaving the subject of guerrilla warfare, I must explain the psychological effect of fighting a guerrilla war. Commonly, in a guerrilla war the regular troops take casualties without ever seeing the enemy, which means without being able to shoot back. Frustrated and enraged, the regulars eventually snap and begin killing anyone they think might be a guerrilla — or might be helping the guerrillas.

In other words, they begin to commit murder. Young men, who only a few months before were living ordinary lives at home with their families, begin to behave like serial killers.

Chris, try to imagine how the troops feel after the heat of the moment when they begin to think about what they have done.

Each such incident further destroys morale, which is a polite way of saying it increases pressure for troops to desert and mutiny.

It gets worse. In every guerrilla war there is a moment when a regular troop gets lucky, kills a guerrilla before the guerrilla can kill him, then turns over the body to find that it is a woman. From that moment on, the regulars know they must kill women, including mothers and teen-age girls.

There is nothing more demoralizing to a male soldier. Once the need to kill women becomes known, morale plunges further, and the army is in serious danger of losing the war.

The Vietnam War was mostly a guerrilla war. U.S. regulars were fighting Vietnamese guerrillas.

You might remember reading about the My Lai massacre in Vietnam. Lt. Calley's platoon had been taking casualties for weeks without being able to retaliate. They finally went crazy and tried to wipe out the whole village of My Lai, every man, woman and child.

Calley and several others were court-martialed and found guilty of murdering 500 innocent people.

The governments of Europe, armed with cannons against bows and arrows, conquered nearly the whole world using the procedure of "kill them all and let God sort them out." This suggestion, which was followed by the Calley group, was heard often in Vietnam.

In Vietnam, many Americans learned the hard way that even a small child can hand you a Coke can with a grenade inside. In 1967, a journalist from Life Magazine asked an army sergeant if there was a way to win the war. The sergeant said, "Kill everyone over five years old."

Again, guerrilla war is mostly about morale. Once a regular troop realizes his job is to be a murderer, he loses the desire to fight and begins to think about desertion and mutiny.

Chris, as I mentioned in an earlier letter, in nearly all cases, guerrillas are entirely defensive, not offensive. They do not invade other countries because they are only part-time soldiers who have civilian jobs and families to take care of.

So it is not a bad generalization to say that if you find yourself fighting a guerrilla, you are on the wrong side. He is not on your territory, you are on his; he is not the invader, you are.

When regular troops figure this out, thoughts of desertion and mutiny sweep through the ranks. No one likes to discover that he is risking his life for purposes that are dishonorable.

The soldier begins to see the officer giving him his orders as the real enemy.

So every knowledgeable officer knows that if he goes into a guerrilla war he runs a high risk of being shot by one of his own soldiers.

Regulars often lose guerrilla wars due to exhaustion. A whole battalion can spend weeks trying to find one sniper. But my guess is that they more often lose because it takes only one angry private to kill a general; the smart generals take early retirements.

The amazing effectiveness of guerrillas can be seen in the Afghan war against the Russians during the 1980s. Early on, the primitive Afghans were armed only with pre-World War I bolt-action rifles. They had to melt lead to make their own bullets, and they ground up old celluloid movie film to use as gunpowder. Yet they made life awful for the Russians and prevented Russian occupation of most of the country.

Later, the Afghans acquired modern weapons including shoulder-launched guided missiles. These enabled them to drive the Russians all the way out of Afghanistan.

That is the key, modern weapons. If the guerrillas can acquire a supply of high quality light weapons, the invader will be in deep trouble.

Think about it, in Afghanistan, guerrilla tactics and modern weapons enabled small bands of primitive tribesmen to defeat the second most powerful nation ever seen on earth.[61]

---

[61] The U.S. was the most powerful.

A militia/guerrilla defense is a porcupine defense. A porcupine is a quiet, peaceful animal, but woe unto anyone who attacks him.

In November 1939, Russia attacked Finland. Russia's population was 190 million; Finland's, four million. The Russians were also superior in every type of weapon: tanks, artillery, planes, and warships.[62]

The Finns had only two advantages. They were fighting on their own territory, which they knew intimately, and they were using guerrilla tactics.

The Finns fought the Russians to a standstill. They did not succeed in ejecting the Russians completely, but they did save most of their country, and the Russians will never forget the horrors they suffered in the Finnish campaign.

For a century or so after the Industrial Revolution, European powers were able to conquer most of the world because they had battleships against bows and arrows, but that window of opportunity is closed now. Most of the world is industrialized, and guerrillas can usually get the modern weapons they need.

They can also travel easily all over the world and strike back in places and ways least expected. They do not like to leave home and family, but, if driven to desperate measures, they will do it. The war that grew out of the September 11th attack on the United States became the world's first global guerrilla war.

Chris, in my next letter we will go back to the Philippines, where Filipinos decided to fight for their

---

[62] STALIN, by Albert Marrin, Puffin Books, a division of the Penguin Group, NY, 1988, p.161-169.

independence and began a guerrilla war. The U.S. conquest of the Philippines was a crucial step toward the World Wars.

Uncle Eric

P.S. As I write this, the USG's war in the Mideast has barely begun, so it is hard to know what to say about it.

I can offer the observation that, so far, U.S. forces have been very reluctant to kill or risk civilians because in Vietnam they learned what happens to morale when civilians are killed.

U.S. officials say often that we should expect the war to go on for years, so it will be interesting to see if U.S. forces find a way to permanently subdue guerillas without massacring non-guerrillas.

As explained in my previous set of letters written before September 11, 2001, about THE THOUSAND YEAR WAR IN THE MIDEAST, the group that attacked on September 11th was angry at the USG's involvement in their countries. They would have liked to use B-52 bombers and aircraft carriers to retaliate against the USG, but they didn't have them, so they used what they had — guerrilla tactics.

Where this global guerrilla war will lead no one can know, but since you have read my 1999 set of letters about the war, you know how it began, and the seventh deadly idea — Manifest Destiny, or Indispensable Nation — played no small part in that beginning. More than a century ago the USG got the idea it had the right to interfere in other parts of the world, and we are still paying the price. More about those early interventions in my next letter.

25

Take No Prisoners

Dear Chris,

In the aftermath of the Spanish-American War, Cubans were allowed to have a degree of self-government, but, like the American Indian tribes, they had no choice about becoming a possession of the USG. Cubans lived on a small island only 90 miles from the U.S., and they knew what had happened to Indians who had resisted the USG. They begrudgingly accepted their fate.

In contrast, Filipinos were given no self-government, and they lived on a group of 7,000 islands that were 5,000 miles from the U.S.

Filipinos decided to fight for their independence and began a guerrilla war.

You cannot shoot what you cannot find. In the Philippine rebellion against the USG, guerrillas attacked U.S. troops at the village of Balangiga on Samar Island, then disappeared. Unable to find or identify them, General Jacob Smith ordered the killing of everyone over ten years old on the whole island.

Small children and babies were spared, but without adults to take care of them, it is reasonable to assume that many of them died, too.

The frustrated General Smith told the troops, "I want no prisoners. I wish you to burn and kill; the more you burn and kill, the better it will please me."[63]

---

[63] ALMANAC OF AMERICA'S WARS by John S. Bowman, Brompton Books, Hong Kong, 1990, p. 101.

In military jargon, **take no prisoners** means kill everyone, even those who wave a white flag to surrender.

After the main Philippine island of Luzon had been taken, President McKinley wondered if he should conquer the other islands.

One evening, McKinley decided yes. Later he explained that, "we could not leave them to themselves, they were unfit for self-government... [so] ...there was nothing left for us to do but to take them all, and to educate the Filipinos, and uplift and civilize and Christianize them, and by God's grace do the very best we could by them, as our fellow-men for whom Christ also died. And then I went to bed, and went to sleep, and slept soundly, and the next morning I sent for the chief engineer of the War Department (our mapmaker), and told him to put the Philippines on the map of the United States."[64]

Incidentally, Chris, Christianity was already well established in the Philippines. McKinley apparently either did not know or did not care. This, in my opinion, has been typical in U.S. foreign policy for two centuries — first get into the war, *then* learn the history of the people you are fighting.

Back to the Filipinos. They did not have modern weapons, so they lost the war.

A book popular at that time was OUR NEW POSSESSIONS by Trumbull White. Sold door to door, this book was a proud survey of the USG's newly conquered peoples and territories.

Americans who read OUR NEW POSSESSIONS thrilled to the descriptions of U.S. troops defeating Philippine guerrillas. In Chapter 20, "War and Peace in the Philippines," White describes "tottering old men and little boys, armed only with knives, huddled in the trenches," and mowed down by the

---

[64] THE NATIONALIZING OF AMERICAN LIFE, 1877-1900, edited by Ray Ginger, Free Press, NY, p.282.

Americans, who were backed by artillery and the warships of Admiral Dewey's fleet, including the 4,200-ton cruiser *Charleston*.[65]

Letters from American soldiers to their families at home described — often with naive pride — the atrocities they were committing. Prisoners were routinely shot, whole villages and towns burned to the ground, and Filipino men, women, and children killed in batches of hundreds.[66] It was essentially the same thing as the U.S. Government had done to the American Indians.

Chris, do you see now why I always emphasize that the country and the government are not the same thing. America is a wonderful country, I would not want to live anywhere else, but the government has often been, well, you get the point.

The final body count in the U.S. conquest of the Philippines was about 220,000 Filipino men, women, and children dead,[67] against about 4,243 Americans killed and 2,818 Americans wounded.[68] The total wounded is not known; good records about wounded, especially enemy wounded, were not kept in those days.

Chris, this slaughter was a carbon copy of European behavior. The USG now had the beginnings of its global empire, and was solidly entrenched as a power that would not hesitate to roll over anyone who got in its way.

Uncle Eric

---

[65] OUR NEW POSSESSIONS, by Trumbull White, W.S. Reeve Publishing Co., Chicago, 1898, p.292-295.

[66] "American Foreign Policy, The Turning Point," by Ralph Raico, THE FAILURE OF AMERICA'S FOREIGN WARS, Richard Ebeling and Jacob Hornberger, Eds., Future of Freedom Foundation, Fairfax, VA 1996, p.63.

[67] WALL STREET JOURNAL, "Death Toll," Nov. 19, 1997, p.1.

[68] THE U.S. AND THE PHILIPPINES, PBS documentary.

26

The White Man's Burden and the Ugly American

Dear Chris,

In 1899, as the USG's armed forces were pounding the Spanish and Filipinos, the Nobel Prize winning author Rudyard Kipling wrote a poem advocating continued U.S. and British conquest of darker-skinned people in far off lands.

Titled "The White Man's Burden," Kipling's poem argued that the virtuous British and American white people had a duty to subjugate and civilize, "new caught sullen peoples, half devil and half child."

Kipling said that going to war against these darker-skinned people in far-off lands was difficult and dangerous, but it had to be done in order to bring these people to a better way of life. The white man had to put an end to "sloth and heathen folly."

The **White Man's Burden** became a popular idea, the justification for the British conquest of nearly a fourth of the world.

As you know, in the U.S. war in the Philippines the U.S. Army and Navy eventually "civilized" 220,000 Filipinos to death. Only 4,000 American deaths occurred.[69] This was considered a worthwhile trade-off.

---

[69] WALL STREET JOURNAL, "Death Toll," Nov. 19, 1997, p.1, and THE U.S. AND THE PHILIPPINES, PBS documentary.

And the Spanish-American War was so popular it was called the "Splendid Little War."

The White Man's Burden was also called **Anglo-Saxonism**.

A key component of Anglo-Saxonism was the corruption of religion to justify murder and conquest.

In 1890, the convention of one of the major churches in the U.S. stated that "the religious destiny of the world is lodged in the hands of the English-speaking people. To the Anglo-Saxon race God seems to have committed the enterprise of the world's salvation."[70]

James H. King, an influential minister from New York, said the "most important lesson in the history of modern civilization is, that God is using the Anglo-Saxon to conquer the world for Christ."[71]

In 1901, another religious leader, Lyman Abbott, justified the killing by saying, "It is said that we have no right to go to a land occupied by a barbaric people and interfere with their life. It is said that if they prefer barbarism they have a right to remain **barbarians**. I deny the right of a barbaric people to retain possession of any quarter of the globe. What I have already said I reaffirm: barbarism has no rights which civilization is bound to respect."[72]

In World War I, white Europeans developed the airplane into a weapon of war, then began using it against poorly-armed Muslims and other darker skinned people in far corners of the globe. The first official report of British aircraft strafing in Iraq said that Muslim men, women, and children

---

[70] A CHRISTIAN AMERICA, by Robert T. Handy, Oxford University Press, NY, 1984, p.92.

[71] A CHRISTIAN AMERICA, by Robert T. Handy, p.91.

[72] A CHRISTIAN AMERICA, by Robert T. Handy, p.109.

were killed indiscriminately from the air — "Many of them jumped into a lake, making a good target for the machine guns."[73]

When a British official asked if using aircraft to massacre civilians, including women, might be wrong, he was told that international law did not protect "savage tribes." Strafing women was okay because native tribes were thought to view a woman as "a piece of property somewhere between a rifle and a cow."[74]

Notice that some of the earliest uses of warplanes under the doctrine of the White Man's Burden, or Anglo-Saxonism, were to conquer Muslims in Iraq — a country the USG considers a leading source of "terrorism" as I write this today.

This insane desire to conquer the world in the name of the Prince of Peace was not in any way a secret conspiracy. It was widely publicized and widely supported. The August 3, 1899, CHRISTIAN INDEX newspaper published in Atlanta boldly proclaimed, "Oh, let the stars and stripes, intertwined with the flag of old England, wave o'er the continents and islands of earth, and through the instrumentality of the Anglo-Saxon race, the kingdoms of this world shall become the kingdoms of our Lord and His Christ."[75]

Chris, the Anglo-Saxonists even drafted Santa Claus into carrying the White Man's Burden. In 2001, at the Crocker Art Museum in Sacramento, California, I visited the Victorian Christmas display of cards, ornaments and other Christmas items from the **Victorian Era** (1837 to 1901).[76]

---

[73] "Death Comes Flying," HARPER'S MAGAZINE, September 2001, p.22
[74] "Death Comes Flying," HARPER'S MAGAZINE, September 2001, p.22
[75] A CHRISTIAN AMERICA, by Robert T. Handy, p.110.
[76] Victorian Christmas, a collection by Dolph Gotelli, Crocker Art Museum, Sacramento, CA, November 11, 2001 to January 6, 2002.

I was surprised to see many Santa Clauses carrying British or American flags. The Victorian Christmas tree had a dozen flags protruding from the top, and the garland was all flags. One illustration showed a flag-carrying Santa standing atop the globe.

Another, a two-page color illustration from HARPER'S MAGAZINE, showed Santa with a flag, and a boy and girl asleep on Christmas Eve. The boy was dreaming not of sugarplums, but of toy soldiers battling Filipinos and other dark-skinned people, including ones dressed as Muslims.

Incidentally, Chris, by the time World War I would arrive, the boy in this illustration would have been the right age to volunteer for the army.

In another part of the boy's dream, a white man carries a black man on his shoulders. Apparently, this signifies the White Man's Burden: after the barbarians have been subdued militarily, they will be lifted up and carried to a better life by the superior white Anglo-Saxons. In a land saturated with Anglo-Saxonism, this would be a fitting Christmas wish, a natural accompaniment to "let there be peace on earth."

Chris, no one in Washington D.C. wants to admit that the White Man's Burden, or Anglo-Saxonism is still with us. To camouflage it, the policy has been broadened and redesignated Washington's Burden.

Today, it is the USG that is "superior" to the rest of the world and saddled with the duty to pacify the "savages" in places such as Kosovo, Indonesia, and the Mideast. Americans of any color can join the armed forces and fight anyone that the USG thinks may be in need of .50 caliber enlightenment.

In an earlier letter, I mentioned former Secretary of State Madeleine Albright. In the words of the WASHINGTON POST, "Albright's frequent, triumphal references to the supremacy of U.S. power and values."[77]

The disgusting practice of killing people in the name of the Prince of Peace has faded, but the new war that began September 11, 2001, is so heavily laced with religion that I wonder if the practice will be revived. Journalist Barbara Olsen was killed in the September 11th attack. Three days later, on the web site townhall.com, her friend Ann Coulter wrote, "We should invade their countries, kill their leaders and convert them to Christianity."

The commander of an Air Force unit in Bagram, Afghanistan uses the radio call sign "El Cid," apparently after the famous Christian warrior El Cid, who defeated Muslims in Spain in 1094. The Army's new mobile artillery system is called the Crusader.

In 1958, a new term entered our language, the Ugly American. From the title of a book by Eugene Burdick and William Lederer, Ugly American referred to the belief that we are superior to the rest of the world and have the right to force our ways onto them. One of the fictitious characters in the book, an ambassador to a Southeast Asian nation, thought of the people of that nation as "little monkeys."

In 2001, the USG was thrown off the United Nation's Human Rights Committee and replaced by the government of Sudan. U.S. officials were told that they were being taught a lesson, not only by their enemies, but also by their allies in Europe who were giving notice that the USG had become too arrogant.[78]

Shortly thereafter, writer Lewis H. Lapham was visiting France where he spent four evenings talking with

[77] "No Clout Where It Counts," by John Lancaster, WASHINGTON POST NATIONAL WEEKEND EDITION, April 17, 2000.

[78] International Pacts Undercut U.S. ...," DEFENSE NEWS, June 3, 2001, p.27.

acquaintances about this slap at the USG. Lapham wrote, tongue in cheek:

> Gradually it occurred to me that the French didn't fully appreciate the doctrine of American innocence, what the first Puritans in the Massachusetts wilderness understood as their special appointment from Providence. Because God had chosen America as the construction site of the earthly Paradise, America's cause was always just and nothing was ever America's fault. Subsequent generations of American prophets and politicians have expressed the belief in different words — America, "the Last, Best Hope of Mankind"; America "the Ark of Safety, the Anointed Civilizer" — but none of the witnesses ever fails to understand that whereas corrupt foreigners commit crimes against humanity, Americans cleanse the world of its impurities. We do so because we have a natural aptitude for the work.[79]

Lapham reports that when an opinion poll asked the French what images came to mind when they thought of America, 67% mentioned "violence" and 66% mentioned "power."

Chris, the White Man's Burden has become Washington's Burden, and the rest of the world is getting tired of it. You will have a better understanding of my next topic — and September 11th — if you keep the White Man's Burden and Washington's Burden in mind.

Uncle Eric

---

[79] "The American Rome," by Lewis H. Lapham, HARPER'S, August 2001, p.33.

Conquests of the
Christian European Powers

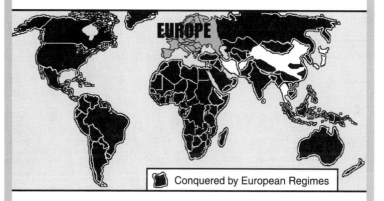

Conquered by European Regimes

In a political sense Christendom is today the world. If we take the map of the globe and mark off the possessions and spheres of influence of the Christian powers, there will be little or nothing left to the independent control of nonChristian governments. The islands of the sea are all appropriated; the Western Continent is wholly under Christian rule; the partition of Africa among the Christian nations of Europe is well-nigh complete; Asia is slowly coming under the control of the Christian nations.

— Quadrennial Address of the Bishops
of the United Brethren Church, 1901
quoted in A CHRISTIAN AMERICA
by Robert T. Handy
Oxford University Press, New York, 1984, p.109

27

The Great White Fleet

Dear Chris,

The next step toward the World Wars was the Great White Fleet.

In 1907, President Theodore Roosevelt sent his Great White Fleet of 16 new battleships around the world to demonstrate that the USG was now a global power.

Notice that the Great White Fleet was not merchant ships or passenger liners, not vessels of peaceful trade and friendship; the Great White Fleet was warships. Its message was not, wherever you are in the world we are looking forward to visiting you and doing business with you. It was, wherever you are, we can kill you.

We can do to you what we did to the Spanish, the Filipinos, and Native Americans.

The Great White Fleet was even more powerful than the one that destroyed the Spanish fleet in Manila. Each battleship, painted white, weighed more than 11,000 tons and carried at least four cannons that could fire shells 12 inches or more in diameter. It could also fire torpedoes and a variety of smaller guns. These were the most advanced weapons of their day.

Loudly cheered all over America, the voyage of the Great White Fleet was the formal announcement that the USG had joined the European game. American rulers, and much of the population, had fully embraced the deadly ideas I have been writing you about: the Pax Romana, fascism, love of political power, global protection, interests, cost externalization, Manifest Destiny, and Anglo-Saxonism or The White Man's Burden.

Chris, now can you see why I say that the ideas and events leading up to the First World War are so important?

I am sure the murder of 220,000 Filipino men, women, and children turns your stomach. But most Americans have never even heard about the USG's conquest of the Philippines. No one ever taught them.

They have been taught to admire the Great White Fleet.

Are you also beginning to understand why so many millions in other countries hate the U.S. Government so much?

Let me emphasize, Chris, neither Cuba, the Philippines, nor Spain were any threat to America. No one was. By the 1890s, America was the undisputed industrial leader of the world. The thought of attacking the U.S. would have been regarded as lunacy in every capitol.

The Spanish-American War and conquest of the Philippines had nothing to do with defense. They were a straightforward grab for territory and taxpayers, justified by the sinking of the *Maine,* and then followed by the threat of the Great White Fleet, justified by the White Man's Burden.

Chris, consider the difference between the Great White Fleet and the Swiss militiaman. Which type of military power do you think is more ethical?

Here is another point to tuck into the back of your mind: from the time of the Great White Fleet on, it was clear to every other government in the world that when they got into a war, it would be a mighty advantage to get the U.S. involved in it — on their side.

Incidentally, what really happened to the *Maine?*

In 1911, the *Maine* was raised and examined. In the 1970s, Admiral Hyman Rickover, the father of the American nuclear submarine fleet, studied the evidence. Rickover said there had been a spontaneous explosion in the coalbunker, an accident common in ships of that era.[80]

Chris, the White Man's Burden, now Washington's Burden, is our eighth deadly idea. Please make an effort to remember it and the seven others. We will eventually cover a total of ten. They are the reason America got into the two World Wars. And, because America won those wars, the ideas are rarely questioned. *Embedded in American culture, these deadly ideas are today the reasons the USG gets into so many wars in far corners of the globe.*

Chris, this is why, in my opinion, the Spanish-American War and conquest of the Philippines were the most important conflicts the U.S. has ever fought. They were small, with few U.S. casualties compared to other wars, but they were when Americans stopped thinking like the 1776 Sons of Liberty — and when they began thinking like the enemy that the Sons of Liberty were fighting, the Europeans.

Uncle Eric

P.S. Theodore Roosevelt, as Assistant Secretary of the Navy, Vice President, and then President, was arguably the most important driving force in America's new desire for global conquests. Roosevelt's most famous remark is that the USG should, "Speak softly and carry a big stick."

---

[80] "CRUCIBLE OF EMPIRE — THE SPANISH-AMERICAN WAR," PBS documentary.

Millions of Americans are tired of that big stick — they have great fear of the government — and on September 11, 2001, we learned that a lot of foreigners are, too.

What could be in the mind of a man who thought it was a fine idea to conquer innocent people in far-off lands?

We will never know, we are not mind readers, but we do know that on his birthday in 1904, the President received a card from Secretary of War Elihu Root, who wrote, "You have made a very good start in life and your friends have great hopes for you when you grow up."[81]

Regarding the taking of Panama, which I will write about shortly, Roosevelt's Attorney General, Philander Knox, told him, "It would be better to keep your action free from any taint of legality."[82] About Roosevelt's ideas for the USG to control the activity of large companies, Supreme Court Justice Oliver Wendell Holmes, Jr. warned that "no part of the conduct of life" would be safe from government interference under such vague principles.[83]

Apparently Roosevelt enjoyed his power and liked to use it as much as possible. A kid with a new toy.

---

[81] "Carrying Sticks and Hugging Trees," by Richard Brookhiser, NEW YORK TIMES BOOK REVIEW, December 9, 2001, p.10.

[82] "Carrying Sticks and Hugging Trees," by Richard Brookhiser, p.10.

[83] "Carrying Sticks and Hugging Trees," by Richard Brookhiser, p.10.

28

Up Close And Personal

Dear Chris,

I need to mention a few final points about guerrilla war before we move on to more events leading to the First World War. Some of this was touched on in my previous set of letters about the Mideast.[84] But the review will be helpful.

Chris, innocent civilians die in every war, sometimes by the millions. In World War II, the British air force **carpet bombed**[85] residential areas of German cities. To keep this from being called terrorism, it was called "**area bombing**[86]."[87]

Guerrilla war tends to limit the killing of civilians and bring an earlier end to the war because the regular troops are forced to see their victims face to face, "up close and personal," sometimes even to touch them. This levies a

---

[84] Uncle Eric is referring to chapters 15 and 20 of THE THOUSAND YEAR WAR IN THE MIDEAST: HOW IT AFFECTS YOU TODAY by Richard J. Maybury, published by Bluestocking Press, web site: www.BluestockingPress.com

[85] Carpet bombing means large numbers of planes laying a carpet of bombs across the target.

[86] Area bombing: a British term from World War II. The bombing of civilian housing areas for the purpose of killing and terrorizing civilian men, women, and children. Done mostly by the British to Germans, but also done to some extent by Americans to Germans, and to a greater extent by Americans to Japanese.

[87] HISTORY OF THE SECOND WORLD WAR, by B.H. Liddell Hart, Perigree Books, New York, 1982, p.594-595.

terrible psychological toll on the regulars, increasing the pressure for desertion and mutiny.

In non-guerrilla war, the two sides often pound each other from great distances, sometimes hundreds of miles. The regulars are detached from their victims and feel little need to rebel against orders. This detached style of warfare became so highly developed in the 20th century that now young officers sit in underground bunkers and submarines ready to pour nuclear fire on tens of millions any time their government tells them to, and this is considered entirely ethical.

Mutiny is most common among ground troops, less so in navies, and I have never heard of a case in an air force.

After the Vietnam War, most cases of **delayed stress syndrome**[88] were among ground troops.

In Vietnam, a new word was invented, **fragging**; it means tossing a fragmentation grenade into an officer's tent by one of his own men. This one word sheds much light on why the U.S. lost in Vietnam and why the Russians lost in Afghanistan and why in the new "War on Terror" American generals are very keen on avoiding civilian deaths. Many of today's generals were officers in Vietnam, and they lived with the constant danger of fragging.

If the Filipinos had owned modern weapons, I am sure the U.S. would have lost in the Philippines, too.

Uncle Eric

---

[88] Delayed stress syndrome: an emotional illness caused by the stress of combat. In World War I, called shell shock. In World War II, battle fatigue.

29

The First Casualty of War

Dear Chris,

As I said, my purpose in writing these letters is to give you the rest of the story about the World Wars, the non-statist side that you are not likely to get anywhere else. I think you can already see how different the non-statist side is. Talk with your friends and relatives, how many of them know anything about the U.S. conquest of the Philippines?

Chris, as I said earlier, the Spanish-American War was more important, in my opinion, than any other since. It was the great precedent. It created the conditions for all the American conflicts that followed, especially the World Wars, but also the Korean, Vietnam, and Iraq-Kuwait Wars, as well as the war that began on September 11, 2001, with the destruction of the World Trade Center. In the Spanish-American War, Americans embraced the belief that the USG has the right and duty to meddle in other countries.

Here is another lesson to be learned from the Spanish-American War — *always be skeptical about reasons for going to war.*

"The first casualty when war comes is truth," said Senator Hiram Johnson in 1917.

People who have **war fever** will grasp at any straw to justify getting into the fight.

Another comment I like is that of Brigadier General Sir Harry Paget Flashman: "There is no sight more inspiring or heartwarming than troops marching out to battle when you are not going with them."

In 1897, the American steamship *Olivette* was about to leave Cuba. Spanish police who were looking for messages from Cuban rebels boarded the ship. The Spanish police suspected three young women of carrying the messages. The women were questioned and searched.

The New York JOURNAL newspaper ran a story about the incident. The headline was "Does Our Flag Protect Women?" Accompanying the story was a vivid graphic sketch by artist Frederic Remington showing a helpless young woman stripped completely naked and searched by three men.

Chris, you can imagine the cry of outrage and calls for revenge from the American public.

A rival newspaper located one of the young women and showed her the JOURNAL's story. She indignantly protested that the story and graphic were misleading. She said that a police matron had searched the women quite properly with no men present.[89]

But by the time the truth was revealed, the damage was done. America had war fever and the Spanish-American War had become all but inevitable.

The use of lies to create war fever has now been developed to a fine art.

In the Iraq-Kuwait War that began in 1990, the American public was solidly against getting into the war until a teenage Kuwaiti girl appeared on TV. She tearfully told of visiting a Kuwaiti hospital when Iraqi troops stormed in to steal incubators and carry them back to Iraq.

---

[89] "The Needless War With Spain," by William E. Leuchtenburg, AMERICAN HERITAGE MAGAZINE, February 1957, p.35.

To the horror and shock of American audiences, the young woman said the soldiers threw babies from the incubators and allowed them to die on the floor. Follow-up reports put the number of babies killed at 312. The story caused a massive shift in public opinion, and America was again swept by war fever. Women, who are normally quick to speak out against war, were silenced by the thought of hundreds of babies murdered.

The intensity of the emotion was so great that after the war began, take-out pizza sales soared; each evening after work, people would come home, order a pizza and watch the war on TV, rooting as if it were a football game.

Only after the war was over did the truth come out. The baby incubator incident never happened.

The girl who said she saw the babies thrown from the incubators was the daughter of the Kuwaiti Ambassador to the U.S. The story had been invented to inflame the passions of the American public, and it certainly worked.

Another lie was told at the beginning of the Vietnam War. You may have heard of the Gulf of Tonkin incident.

On August 4, 1964, President Lyndon Johnson called congressional leaders to an emergency meeting in the White House Cabinet room. Johnson shocked the members of Congress with the announcement that North Vietnamese warships in the Tonkin Gulf had attacked the U.S. destroyers *Maddox* and *Turner Joy.*

Pleading for congressional backing for retaliation against North Vietnam, Johnson said, "some of our boys are floating around in the water." This created in the minds of the members of Congress the image of ships ablaze and sailors struggling in oil-slicked waves.[90]

---

[90] "The Phantom Battle That Led To War," U.S. NEWS & WORLD REPORT, July 23, 1984, p.64.

The shaken members of Congress quickly advised their colleagues to support retaliation.

On August 7, 1964, Congress passed the Gulf of Tonkin Resolution, which was a blank check for Johnson to go to war.

The truth did not come out until years later.

In the Gulf of Tonkin, vessels from the South Vietnamese and North Vietnamese navies had been fighting, and the two U.S. destroyers had been sent into the middle of it.

Fast action by the ships' crews enabled them to evade the danger. A single machine gun bullet had struck the *Maddox,* making a half-inch hole and scratching the paint.[91] That was the only damage. No sailor had been harmed and none were in the water except in the sense that they were on ships that were in the water.

But, in Washington D.C., caution had been erased by war fever. No one asked for proof that the ships had been sunk. And, apparently, no one even bothered to ask why the U.S. ships were in a known war zone in the first place.

When we get to the U.S. entry into World War I, you will learn about the sinking of the passenger liner *Lusitania.* This was another case of truth being the first casualty of war.

Uncle Eric

P.S. Chris, the "exaggeration" during a war sometimes goes on long afterward. In his memoirs of World War II, Britain's Prime Minister Winston Churchill wrote that the Germans had at least a thousand heavy tanks in 1940. The fact is that in 1940 the Germans had no heavy tanks at all. A heavy tank

---

[91] "The Phantom Battle That Led To War," U.S. NEWS & WORLD REPORT, July 23, 1984, p.59.

weighed at least 30 tons; the German Royal Tiger weighed 70 tons, but didn't make an appearance in the war until 1944, and even then, only 489 saw service. In 1940 the Germans had a few medium tanks weighing barely 20 tons, and the rest were light tanks. Contrary to what is still widely believed, the French at that time had more and better tanks than the Germans.[92]

These days no one talks about telling lies or exaggerating to justify getting into wars. They talk about "building national consensus."

The Swiss clean and oil their rifles, and watch the massacres, shaking their heads as they have for centuries.

---

[92] HISTORY OF THE SECOND WORLD WAR by B.H. Liddell Hart, Perigee Books, NY, 1982, p.19-21.

30

Stealing Panama

Dear Chris,

At the peak of the war in the Philippines, the USG had 70,000 troops stationed there. The final American body count was 4,243 killed and 2,818 wounded.

U.S. leaders got away with it, so after the Spanish-American War and conquest of the Philippines, the practice of using American military personnel for reasons other than the defense of America was solidly entrenched, and it remains so.

The next noteworthy U.S. military action — the one that tested the Philippine precedent — was the Panama incident.

The USG wanted to build the Panama Canal. Panama was a part of Columbia, and the Colombian senate refused to lease the land on terms the USG hoped for.

A Panamanian rebellion against the Colombian government had been blowing hot and cold for decades, and the Panamanians were angry with Columbia's Senate for rejecting the USG's offer.

The rebellion heated up, and the Colombian government attempted to send troops to put it down.

On November 2, 1903, President Theodore Roosevelt ordered a squadron of warships led by the cruiser *Nashville* to help the rebels.

U.S. Marines invaded the Panamanian city of Colon.

The warships and Marines held the Colombian forces at bay, enabling the rebels to win the war. The rebels declared independence and set up their own government.

On November 11th, this new government, which had, in effect, been created by the USG, signed the Panama Canal Treaty allowing the USG to build the canal.

Little Colombia did not have a prayer of defending itself against the mighty U.S., so the victory stood, thereby cementing the notion that American troops should be used for purposes that have nothing to do with defending America. Indeed, the victory cemented America's marriage to all ten deadly ideas, including the eight we have covered so far:

1.   The Pax Romana. America should use its military might to force peace onto other parts of the world.

2.   Fascism. America should do whatever appears necessary, no exceptions, no limits, even to the point of attacking countries that have done no harm to America.

3.   Love of political power. What is the point of having political power, including military power, if you cannot use it on someone?

4.   Global protection. The armed forces should be used abroad to protect Americans who choose to travel or do business — or build canals — in high risk areas.

5.   Interests. The Panama Canal was an "interest" deemed to be worth risking the lives of American soldiers and sailors.

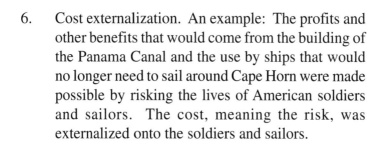

6.   Cost externalization. An example: The profits and other benefits that would come from the building of the Panama Canal and the use by ships that would no longer need to sail around Cape Horn were made possible by risking the lives of American soldiers and sailors. The cost, meaning the risk, was externalized onto the soldiers and sailors.

7.   Manifest Destiny. Americans are superior to other people and have the right to conquer them and make them part of the American Empire.

8.   The White Man's Burden (or Anglo-Saxonism). The white English-speaking Christian American is a superior form of human and has the right and duty to force his ways onto others.

       As for the other two deadly ideas — alliances and the glory of war — I have not explained them yet, but you can see them in the Panama incident. The USG formed an alliance with the Panamanian rebels, and Americans thrilled to the glory of the victory. More about these two deadly ideas later.
       Chris, in 1977, the USG was debating whether to give up the Panama Canal. Some said the canal had to be turned over to the Panamanians because the U.S. had no right to it in the first place. This is when Senator S.I. Hayakawa of California made his famous remark, "It's ours! We stole it fair and square!"

                                   Uncle Eric

31

Helping Crooks and Tyrants

Dear Chris,

I'd like to make one more point before we get more deeply into the ideas and events that led to the World Wars.

America is a very frustrating place for a powerseeker, thanks to the precautions taken by James Madison and the other American Founders.

Inside the U.S., people are protected from the government by the Constitution, especially the Bill of Rights. These protections have been severely eroded, but they remain strong enough to be highly annoying to a powerseeker.

However, Chris, and this is crucially important to remember, the Bill of Rights stops at the border. Outside the country, a powerseeker can do anything he pleases.

This was the message of the Spanish-American War, the conquest of the Philippines, the taking of Panama, and the Great White Fleet. Outside the U.S. there are few limits to the USG's power.

These four precedents between 1898 and 1907 set the stage for the rest of American history.

This is one of the chief reasons so many millions of foreigners hate the U.S. Government. During the 20th century, every President sent American troops to far corners of the globe, usually not to defend liberty, but to train, equip, or provide other kinds of help to the armed forces of crooks and tyrants. These crooks and tyrants have included, but are not limited to: President Diem of Vietnam, the Shah of Iran, Marcos in the Philippines, Manuel Noriega in Panama, Saddam Hussein in Iraq, Mobutu in the Congo, Chiang Kai-shek in Taiwan, General Park in Korea, and Suharto and Habibie in Indonesia.

Research the biographies of these crooks and tyrants, Chris, and remember, they all received help from the USG. As I said in an earlier letter, during the 20th century, U.S. forces were sent abroad into harm's way no less than 188 times,[93] and dozens of these times were to help keep in power people you would not want to meet in a dark alley.

Nearly any foreign thug who promises to be part of the USG's so-called "sphere of influence" — meaning the USG's Empire — receives military assistance that is usually used to suppress his own people. The Shah of Iran and his secret police, for instance, terrorized Iranians for 25 years with the backing of the USG. The Shah received highly advanced U.S. weapons, military training, and military intelligence information.

In September 1999, in the TV news clips of Indonesian troops slaughtering unarmed Christians in East Timor, you may have noticed that the Indonesian troops carried American weapons. The USG had given the Muslim government of Indonesia three billion of our tax dollars knowing full well that 200,000 Christians were being murdered.

There are about 220 countries in the world. As I write this, the USG has 280,000 troops stationed in 138 of them, from Antigua to Zimbabwe,[94] about two-thirds of all countries.

---

[93] U.S. Navy official web site, and "Presidents Have A History...," by L. Gordon Crovitz, WALL STREET JOURNAL, January 15, 1987, p.24.

[94] NAVY TIMES, February 14, 2000, p.12.

All these American troops are providing some kind of help to the governments of these countries. *All these governments have enemies, so now their enemies are our enemies.* This is part of the legacy of the events that led up to World War I. Now you know why I call them the ten *deadly* ideas.

Speaking of Indonesia, in 2001, the National Security Archive, a nonprofit research institute at George Washington University in Washington D.C., obtained a copy of a State Department book about U.S. involvement in Indonesia during the 1960s.[95] Publication of the untitled book was banned by the State Department, but the book was posted at www.nsarchive.org and may still be there.

The book reveals that during a rebellion against the dictatorial Indonesian government, the U.S. State Department supplied military units with money and intelligence information about suspected rebels. This led to the deaths of more than 100,000 suspects.

Chris, note the word "suspects." Not convicted criminals, suspects. The Indonesian government has never been very big on legal technicalities such as evidence and juries.

This is the kind of atrocity the USG's aid has helped create in country after country for at least a hundred years.

Chris, check the legal systems of countries around the world. I provided that information to you in my previous set of letters on economics.[96] Another good place to start is the CIA's web site.

---

[95] "Book on U.S. Role...," CHICAGO TRIBUNE, July 29, 2001, p.6.

[96] Uncle Eric is referring to pages 107-123, "Nations and Legal Systems," in WHATEVER HAPPENED TO PENNY CANDY by Richard J. Maybury, published by Bluestocking Press, web site: www.BluestockingPress.com

You will find only about 20 countries where an American would feel comfortable living if he had to give up his American citizenship and live under the laws as the natives do. That's 20 out of about 220. Most of the world is a nasty place and always has been.

The USG gives assistance to 138 of these governments.

For a list of governments receiving weapons or other largess financed by your tax dollars see the Amnesty International web site: www.amnesty-usa.org/stoparms/countries.html. For the human rights abuse report in which the State Department is forced to admit what they know about these governments: www.state.gov/g/drl/rls/hrrpt/2001. You might also check the STATISTICAL ABSTRACT OF THE UNITED STATES, or WORLD ALMANAC, the Freedom Scale on the Freedom House web site (www.freedomhouse.org), and the Index of Economic Freedom on the Heritage Foundation web site (www.heritage.org). (Web sites change often. If you can no longer access these addresses you might try an internet search).

You will find that the USG is providing assistance to a lot of vicious people.

Chris, do not be misled by the term "economic" aid. Money is **fungible**. This means one dollar can substitute for any other dollar.

Each dollar provided to the government of, say, Egypt, to buy blankets is a dollar the Egyptian government does not need to spend on blankets, so it is a dollar freed up for the Egyptian government to buy bullets.

This U.S. support for the Egyptian dictatorship is one of the many reasons behind the September 11th attack on America. Egyptian authorities have terrorized thousands of innocent people, and all these people have family and friends who are not happy about it. For a look at the behavior of the Egyptian dictatorship — a close ally of the USG — check the Amnesty International web site.

Also, we would be very naive to assume a lot of the U.S. tax money poured into these crooked governments does not end up in the private bank accounts of the rulers.

As you do this research, Chris, keep in mind that the USG's "sphere of influence" did not spring up overnight. It began during the Barbary Wars with the assumption that the USG should protect people who choose to travel in high-risk areas or invest in high-risk areas. It came to full flower a hundred years later during the Spanish-American War. The Spanish-American War then sowed the seeds that led to America's involvement in the two World Wars.

Chris, I think you can see now why I said that by the time you finish reading this set of letters, you will understand many things that even well-informed Americans know little about.

In my opinion, out of all the deadly ideas that lead to war, the standout is the love of political power. This power is what sets government apart from all other institutions.

If you haven't read Dr. Seuss' anti-fascist story YERTLE THE TURTLE,[97] I recommend you do so. As you read it, ponder this question: what is the point of having political power if you cannot use it on someone?

Uncle Eric

---

[97] YERTLE THE TURTLE AND OTHER STORIES by Dr. Seuss, published by Random House, New York, 1950.

32

The Usual Suspects

Dear Chris,

I have spent dozens of letters explaining the ideas and events that led to the World Wars. My focus has been mostly on the view from America. World War I was global, so now we need to move on to a broader view.

In his head every police officer carries a list of names he calls the Usual Suspects. When the officer gets a report of a fight at a nearby tavern, his list of Usual Suspects immediately comes to mind.

The officer will question this group knowing there is a high probability one or more was involved directly, or indirectly by goading someone else into the fight.

If you look back over the past 500 years of history you will find we can compile a list of Usual Suspects among governments.

To illustrate, if you hear that a huge war has broken out, which governments immediately come to mind?

Do you think of those in Buenos Aries, Alma-Ata, or Rio de Janeiro? How about Canberra? Ottawa? Mexico City?

Or do you think of Moscow, Berlin, Paris, Tokyo, or London?

The first group, the group you did not think of, are all capitals of nations that are large, either in population or territory, and so are highly important, but we do not think of them when we think of wars. They rarely get into wars.

The governments we do think of are the Usual Suspects — Moscow and so forth.

Of the roughly 220 national governments in the world, only a handful qualify for the list of Usual Suspects. In alphabetical order, they are Beijing, Berlin, London, Moscow, Paris, Rome, Tokyo, Vienna, and Washington D.C.

Until the 20th century, all the Usual Suspects were in the Old World. The USG was a latecomer. In the Spanish-American War and conquest of the Philippines, the USG joined the group, making a total of nine Usual Suspects.

If you browse through the past 500 years, whenever you read about a big war, you always find at least one of these nine directly in the fight or helping to fund or instigate it. I know of no exception.

Berlin was also a latecomer (remember, Germany was not a country until 1871).

The government in Vienna faded from importance as Berlin rose, so I do not think it should be regarded as an active member of the group today, although it was responsible for a huge amount of bloodshed for centuries, and the ideas that led to this behavior are certainly not dead in Vienna. Call Vienna a Usual Suspect — retired.

This is not to say that the hundreds of governments that are not on our list of Usual Suspects are saints and angels. They certainly are not, and some are quite bloodthirsty.

In fact, some have been in so many wars that they might be close to qualifying for the list of Usual Suspects. Ankara (Turkey), Islamabad (Pakistan), and New Delhi (India) come to mind. But none have the intensely bloody record that the Usual Suspects do.

In his excellent study of the true behavior of governments, called DEATH BY GOVERNMENT, professor R.J. Rummel lists the worst killers of the 20th century. The top six were leaders of the Usual Suspects: Stalin, Mao Tse-Tung, Hitler, Chiang Kai-shek, Lenin, and Tojo.[98]

All the Usual Suspects were major players in both World Wars, with the exception of Beijing, which had only a minor role in World War I.

Why have the Usual Suspects so often been embroiled in wars?

This is the group that has most enthusiastically embraced the deadly ideas that lead to war.

Chris, all governments embrace these ideas to some extent, but the Usual Suspects have swallowed them hook, line, and sinker.

The Usual Suspects gave us both World Wars, which were the worst wars in history.

Whenever you hear about a new war erupting today, it is a good bet that at least one of the Usual Suspects is in it, or has helped set the stage for it, or is backing one or more of the combatants with money, weapons, intelligence information, or something else. The word neutrality is not in the vocabulary of the Usual Suspects.

For instance, as I write this today, the Arab-Israeli conflict has been in the news continually for more than a half-century. The British government set the stage for it in 1917, and the U.S. Government has had its fingers in it for decades.

Let me explain further.

In World War I, the British took Palestine away from Turkey. In 1917, with little understanding of the people they had decided to rule, British officials issued the Balfour

---

[98] DEATH BY GOVERNMENT, by R.J. Rummel, Transaction Publishers, New Brunswick, NJ, 1994, p.8.

Declaration. This said that a "national home for the Jewish people" should be created in Palestine.

The British did not say what "national home" meant. The Jews took it to mean a Jewish country with a Jewish government.

Naturally, the Muslims who lived on the land did not want to live under a Jewish government. Hatred between the two groups escalated sharply.

By 1948, fighting had grown so intense that the British abandoned Palestine, leaving the two groups to plunge into a full-blown war. The Jews and Muslims have been at it ever since.

In short, the British government lit the fuse on the powder keg, then ran away.

Examine the history of any war raging today. Odds are high that you will find, somewhere in the past, one or more of the Usual Suspects responsible for lighting fuses as London did in Palestine.

The Usual Suspects behave the way they do because they think the way they do. They believe in most or all of the deadly ideas that lead to war.

Chris, each time a war breaks out, imagine yourself as a police officer and ask, which of the Usual Suspects is behind this one? Check the history of the people who are fighting. It will make for an interesting research project.

Uncle Eric

33

Boxer Rebellion and Russo-Japanese War

Dear Chris,

Let's look at two more events that led to World War I — the Boxer Rebellion and the Russo-Japanese War.

The Japanese and Chinese have always had the strange idea that the Orient should belong to the people who live there. Imagine.

Western rulers did not share this belief; and, by 1897, they had conquered most of China.

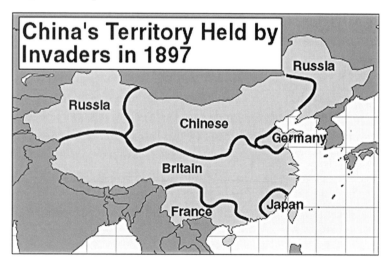

In 1898, the Chinese rebelled against foreign rule. Militia units called *Yihequan*, which means "righteous and harmonious fists," spearheaded the rebellion. The name led to the foreign press calling the rebels the Boxers.

The Boxers rolled across China killing foreigners and anyone suspected of sympathizing with foreigners.

A military force of British, French, German, Japanese, Russian, and U.S. troops was dispatched to China. They entered Beijing in August 1900, and, using vastly superior weapons, put down the rebellion.

But that wasn't the end of the bloodshed. The governments in Moscow and Tokyo both wanted Manchuria and Korea, and were willing to fight over them.

On February 8, 1904, the Japanese fleet launched a surprise attack on the Russian fleet at the Chinese city of Port Arthur (now called Lushun). This was the beginning of the Russo-Japanese War.

Despite the construction of the Trans-Siberian Railroad, the Russians were unable to get enough troops and equipment to Manchuria to beat the Japanese.

In May 1905, a Russian fleet that had sailed all the way from the Baltic was met by the Japanese and destroyed.

The Russo-Japanese War was the first conflict in modern times in which an Asian power defeated a European power (the Mongols had done it during the Middle Ages). This war can be seen as the beginning of the Japanese attempt to copy what the U.S. had done in the Spanish-American War — that is, to start building its own empire by stealing territory from the people who had stolen it first, the Europeans.

Another point to keep in mind is that in Western history books the Boxer Rebellion and Russo-Japanese War have often been painted as treachery on the part of the Chinese and Japanese. The question to ask is, who was on whose territory? Had the Japanese and Chinese invaded the West, or had the West invaded the Orient?

Uncle Eric

34

Choosing Up Sides

Dear Chris,

Prussia's Count Otto von Bismark knew a lot about the behavior of people in the Old World. He had a saying: "A generation that has taken a beating is always followed by a generation that deals one."[99]

Think about it, Chris. If the second generation deals one, then someone else is taking that beating, and they will be followed by a generation that deals one, and so forth forever.

That's the Old World, and it is why America's Founders advised us never to get involved in the quarrels of the Old World. Once in, it is very difficult to get back out, the hatreds never end.

Unfortunately, the Founders did not follow their own advice. They got into the Barbary Wars, and because of that, we are still entangled in the Old World's conflicts. As you know from my previous set of letters about the THE THOUSAND YEAR WAR IN THE MIDEAST, the September 11th attacks on the United States can be traced directly to the U.S. involvement in the Barbary Wars over two centuries ago.

The Founders were human and made mistakes. Sometimes it is better to admire them for what they taught, not what they did.

[99] HISTORY OF WORLD WAR I, by General S.L.A. Marshall, American Heritage, NY 1982, p.22.

One of the worst of the Old World's conflicts was World War I. In terms of the number of people killed, only World War II surpassed it.

Here are more of the events that led to World War I.

After losing the Franco-Prussian War of 1870, the French began to rebuild their armed forces. One objective was to regain the provinces of Alsace and Lorraine that had been taken by the Germans.

Chris, I have visited Alsace and Lorraine and found them to be a charming blend of French and German culture and language. They have changed hands so many times that you can walk into one bakery and think you are in France, then walk up the block into another bakery and think you are in Germany.

The town of Kayserberg is just down the road from Col du Bonhomme.

You should not be surprised in Alsace and Lorraine if you meet a woman named Gigi married to a man named Heinz.

This, incidentally, is common in the Old World in areas along borders. I once visited a town on the border between Austria and Italy where the people got tired of changing the language of the street signs every time the town changed hands. Now all signposts have two signs, one in each language. Imagine trying to follow a map in a town where every street has two names, one Austrian and one Italian.

You are no doubt familiar with the movie THE SOUND OF MUSIC about the von Trapp family's escape from Austria. The von Trapps did not really escape over the mountains to Switzerland as presented in the Hollywood version of the story. Historian William Anderson discloses in his book THE WORLD OF THE TRAPP FAMILY, "Although the von Trapps were Austrians, a technicality made them Italian citizens. Their former home at Trieste had been turned over to Italy after World War I, so they held Italian passports. This enabled them to leave Austria freely...they headed for St. Georgen in Northern Italy. With their Italian passports, the Nazis could do them no harm."[100] Italy was an ally of Germany. This is an example of how Europeans have so often found themselves displaced by politics and wars.

After the Franco-Prussian War the Germans saw the French rearming and got worried. Chris, try to follow this on a map or globe.

Germans and Austrians speak the same language and are close cousins culturally. The Austro-Hungarian Empire was an ancient enemy of the French Empire, so the Germans and Austro-Hungarians formed an alliance. This alliance became the cornerstone of what would eventually become the Central Powers in World War I.

The Italians also did not like the French having been invaded by them in the past, so they joined Germany and Austria-Hungary, forming the so-called Triple Alliance, which became the core of the Central Powers.

This was also the core of the Axis in World War II.

In both World Wars, Italy switched sides, joining the Allies. This is a common practice in the Old World; governments often welsh on agreements and stab each other in the back. If a war is not going in a direction they like, they make whatever changes they think will get them what they want. If this requires betraying their allies, so be it.

The Russians and the Austro-Hungarian Empire had a long history of competition for land and taxpayers, and they did not have much good to say about each other. Feeling a

---

[100] THE WORLD OF THE TRAPP FAMILY SINGERS by William Anderson, published by Anderson Publications, PO Box 423, Davison, MI. pg. 56.

threat from the Triple Alliance, the Kremlin formed an alliance with Paris.

Sandwiched between the French and the Russians, the Germans got even more worried and began building up their armed forces, including their naval fleet.

Britain is an island nation and has long relied on its navy as its main fighting force. The buildup of the German navy worried the British, so they joined the French and Russians. These three became the core of the group called the Allies.

They were also the core of the Allies in World War II.

It was the same thing as children in a school yard forming gangs. Each gang of Usual Suspects was afraid of the other and tried to recruit more members and gather more weapons. That is the Old World; they have been behaving this way for thousands of years.

One member recruited by the Russians was Serbia. Regarding Serbia as its "little Slavic sister," the Kremlin pledged that if the Serbs would join the Russia-France-Britain alliance (Allies), Russia would protect the Serbs against the Austrians.

Ties between Serbia and Russia are ancient; both are Eastern Orthodox Christian, and they have long fought together against Turks, who are Muslim.

Summarizing, by 1914, Europe was divided into two gangs, the Allies and the Central Powers. Three of the Usual Suspects led one gang, and three led the other. Both sides were furiously building weapons and training troops.

Over the past several thousand years, these nations and their ancestors had been down this road hundreds of times, so it did not take a genius to see what was coming. This is just one more example of why Thomas Jefferson referred to the Europeans as "nations of eternal war."

Uncle Eric

35

The Morocco Crisis

Dear Chris,

As I mentioned in an earlier letter, thousands of books, screenplays, and articles have been written about the World Wars. In any library or encyclopedia you can find exhaustive details of the events. My purpose here is not to repeat what you can easily find in these other sources, but to give you a way to understand it, to sort the wheat from the chaff.

The formation of the two gangs in Europe did not keep the Europeans from continuing to conquer the rest of the world.

Chris, here are more events leading up to World War I.

The French already had Algeria and, in 1905, decided they also wanted Morocco. The Germans did not like any expansion of French power, so they tried to block French moves toward Morocco.

The French and German governments rattled their sabers at each other. The Germans decided Morocco was not worth fighting for, so they backed down.

In 1907, the French attacked Morocco and proceeded to conquer it piece by piece.

Not surprisingly, the Moroccans did not like French rule, and in 1911 they rebelled.

To protect Germans in Morocco, the German government sent the gunboat *Panther* to Morocco. Remember the deadly idea of global protection.

Morocco Crisis
The Results

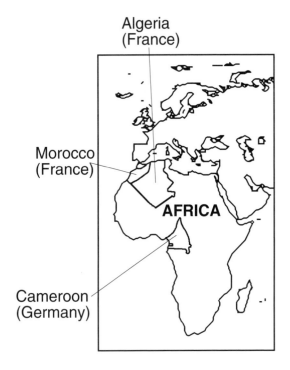

The French government had already conquered Algeria, and the German government did not want them to also have Morocco. The British came to the aid of the French, and the two together intimidated the Germans into backing down. The French yielded parts of Cameroon to the Germans as a consolation prize.

The French saw the *Panther* as a threat to their control of Morocco. Remember the deadly idea of interests.

With the French and Germans facing off, the British came to the aid of their French allies and rattled their saber at the Germans. The Germans again backed down, with an agreement. The French government could own Morocco and the Moroccans, and the Germans would get land and people in Black equatorial Africa; this would become part of the German government's Cameroon.

Like the Moroccans, the black Africans were not asked if they wanted to be ruled by the Europeans. The Europeans had superior weapons, and this was all that mattered. The French gave the Africans and their land to the Germans, and the Africans became German subjects.

This was typical all over the world. The Europeans carved up the globe, playing with the land and the people living on it, as if these people were so many tokens on a board game. Chris, always keep in mind that each of the millions of people killed by the Europeans was a living, breathing human being who was deeply loved by someone.

In the Moroccan Crisis, the French and Germans had no shoot-out, but their customary hatred had grown. And the British alliance with the French against the Germans had been strengthened.

Chris, if you ever travel to Europe, I hope you will take time to talk with the people who live there. Ask what they think of their neighbors in nearby countries. You might be surprised to find that the antagonisms from previous centuries are alive and well. The Old World changes on the surface, but underneath, the hatreds are not a lot different than they were a thousand years ago. Nor, in many areas, is the bigotry.

Uncle Eric

36

Alliances

Dear Chris,

Now we come to the Balkans.

In the 1300s, the Turks, who are Muslim, conquered the Balkans.

The Balkans are Slovenia, Croatia, Bosnia, Montenegro, Kosovo, Macedonia, Albania, Greece, Bulgaria, Serbia, Romania, and Turkey.

In October 1912, the Christian states of Montenegro, Serbia, Bulgaria, and Greece declared war on the Turks. They won, throwing the Turks out.

In 1913, the Bulgarians said they had done the most work to beat the Turks and they deserved a reward. They wanted Macedonia, and they went to war to get it.

The Serbs and Greeks, who did not want the Bulgarians in their backyards, beat them.

Desiring an empire like those of the Usual Suspects, the Serbian government had long sought to expand its control of the Balkans. Having beaten the Bulgarians, the Serbs were feeling confident.

Rulers of Austria wanted land and taxpayers in the Balkans, too, and they were maneuvering to get them. The Serbs did not like this.

On June 28, 1914, the heir to the Austro-Hungarian throne, Archduke Franz Ferdinand, was shot and killed by a Serb in Sarajevo, Bosnia.

The Austrian government accused the Serbian government of having instigated the killing. On July 19th the Austrian Ministerial Council decided that Serbia would be "beaten to earth."[101]

On July 23rd the Austrian government delivered an ultimatum. The Serbs must formally condemn all anti-Austrian propaganda, expel from office anyone suspected of anti-Austrian activity, and allow Austrian police to come onto Serbian soil and suppress anti-Austrian activity.

The Serbs refused to submit to this, so on July 28th Austria-Hungary declared war on them. The next day, Austrian artillery began to bombard Belgrade, the capital of Serbia.

---

[101] HISTORY OF WORLD WAR I, by General S.L.A. Marshall, American Heritage, NY 1982, p.27.

Then the dominoes began to fall. Serbia's ally, Russia, immediately began to **mobilize**.[102]

Austria's ally, Germany, saw this and declared war on Russia.

Russia's ally, France, began to mobilize, which prompted Germany to declare war on France.

Then France's ally, Britain, declared war on Germany.

Chris, one of the most important lessons to learn from World War I is that alliances turn small wars into big ones. Because of the alliances formed by the Usual Suspects, the killing of one man, Archduke Ferdinand, created a chain reaction that brought all of Europe's major powers into battle.

Alliances are the ninth deadly idea that leads to war.

Let me emphasize, Chris, they all went to war because they had promised each other that they would. They had formed alliances. This small war became World War I because of alliances. It had nothing to do with good versus evil. Think of a barroom brawl. A fight starts between two people.

The main thing people learn from history is that they do not learn from history. The danger of alliances was clearly demonstrated in World War I; then promptly forgotten. Two decades later, the Usual Suspects did the same thing all over again, forming alliances that led to a chain reaction, which is now called World War II. We will get more deeply into that in my next set of letters about that war.[103]

---

[102] Mobilization: to prepare for war, especially to move forces in the direction of the enemy, but not to cross onto their soil. Crossing onto their soil is the next step, invasion.

[103] Uncle Eric is referring to part two of his world war series, WORLD WAR II: THE REST OF THE STORY by Richard J. Maybury, published by Bluestocking Press, web site: www.BluestockingPress.com

Incidentally, Chris, let me point out that after World War II, the U.S. Government formed many new alliances, some of them with the governments of Israel, Saudi Arabia, Egypt, and other powers in the Mideast. These alliances then led to the war that began on September 11, 2001. You have read my previous set of letters about THE THOUSAND YEAR WAR IN THE MIDEAST so you already know about this.

Uncle Eric

P.S. Chris, I have mentioned that, as I write this, the Swiss have not been in a foreign war in nearly two centuries. The Swiss have been intensely neutral and have had no military alliances.

One reason often cited by the USG's politicians (and many historians) to form alliances is that other nations are too small to defend themselves.

The Swiss, who have a strong militia, had no alliances during the wars of the 19th and 20th centuries. Why did the other countries?

I believe the answer is that few of these other countries have serious militias.

Why don't they?

My guess is that their rulers are afraid to let the people have guns. The rulers know that if their people were armed, the governments would be overthrown. In World War I, after the Russian people acquired guns, they overthrew the Czar and killed him; no national leader is ever likely to forget that. The more oppressive a government is, the less it wants its people to be able to defend themselves.

37

The Glory of War

Dear Chris,

I stated in an earlier letter that the strategies and battles of World War I are not all that important to our present discussion. World War I was just one more case of the governments of the Old World behaving the way they always have.

I should, however, point out the importance of one weapon — the machine gun. It changed the face of war and helped create the conditions that led to the Treaty of Versailles,[104] which led to World War II.

In the American Civil War, gun makers had developed the Gatling gun. The Gatling gun was one of the first attempts to fire bullets in a stream, like water out of a hose. By 1914, much smaller, faster-firing guns than the Gatling gun had been invented, and both sides had them.

Both sides also used the same tactics, infantry charges like those of earlier wars. Lines of men with rifles would rush at each other, as they had been doing in Europe for centuries. (Visual examples of this style of fighting can be seen in the movies GETTYSBURG with Tom Berenger and THE PATRIOT with Mel Gibson.)

The machine guns mowed them down like wheat cut by a scythe.

---

[104] Versailles is pronounced Ver-Sigh. Outside Paris, Versailles is a palace where the treaty was created.

During the first three weeks of World War I, a half-million men were killed or wounded. Yet month after month, year after year, the generals continued sending millions of young men charging into the teeth of the machine guns.

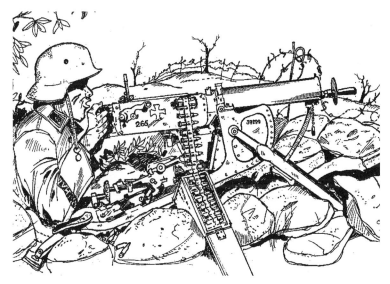

It was not just the generals who demonstrated terrible judgment; it was the young men themselves. This was the same mentality we saw in the Spanish-American War. All across Europe, and then later in America, to the sound of bands and stirring speeches, young men volunteered by the thousands to get into the fight.

The glory of war.

In the first day of the First Battle of the Somme, the British alone had 19,000 killed and 41,000 wounded. The glory of war.

A century earlier, a highly trained soldier with a musket could fire three shots per minute. By 1914, a highly trained soldier with a rifle could fire 15 rounds per minute.

A soldier with a machine gun could fire 600 rounds per minute.[105]

The only defense against this hail of lead was to dig trenches in the direction of the enemy, getting as close as possible. The soldiers would then jump from the trenches and charge, in hopes that they could run past the machine guns before they were cut down. (Examples of this type of slaughter can be seen in the movies ADVENTURES OF YOUNG INDIANA JONES, CHAPTER 8, THE TRENCHES OF HELL and ALL QUIET ON THE WESTERN FRONT. As you watch the World War I soldiers attempt to gain ground amid a hail of machine gun fire, ask yourself, "What 'cause' would make me want to face such slaughter?")

All across Europe, the two sides dug thousands of miles of trenches. The trenches then collected rainwater, and the soldiers lived in the mud at the bottom of the trenches. Disease became an enemy as deadly as the machine guns. Millions watched their skin eaten away by fungus. The glory of war.

If soldiers could get into the enemy's trenches, they suddenly had a face-to-face shoot-out at close quarters. The solution for this was the portable machine gun.

The early machine guns sat on tripods or bipods. They were heavy and awkward to move.

The BAR (Browning Automatic Rifle) and similar guns carried less ammunition and were slower firing but could easily be carried from trench to trench.

The preferred technique was to stand at one end of a trench and fire along the length of it. Hence these portable machine guns came to be known as **trench sweepers**. The glory of war.

---

[105] A HISTORY OF WARFARE, by John Keegan, Vintage Books, Random House, NY, 1993, p.362.

Young men died by the millions, as politicians gave speeches about their heroism.

After they got into the war, the naive soldiers found out what the glory of war was really all about. In protest, French soldiers would baa like sheep going to slaughter as they were marched into the trenches.[106]

Other new weapons were important, too: tanks, aircraft, submarines, and poison gas, among others. (All good research projects. How did they affect World War II?) But nothing so characterized World War I like the endless lines of young men — all deeply loved by mothers, sisters, or wives — massacred by the machine guns, their bodies stacked like cords of firewood rotting in the mud.

Sometimes the bodies could not be stacked. The thousands of heavy artillery pieces bombarding the trenches churned the earth like a giant egg beater. Often not enough of a body could be found to identify it, and thousands were completely buried and never located.

Near Ypres in Belgium is a memorial with 54,900 names of men whose bodies were never found after fighting in a place called the Salient.

At nearby Tyne Cot is another memorial with 34,888 names of those that could not be found. The glory of war.

By November 1918, France alone had 1,700,000 dead from a total population of 40,000,000. In Germany, Britain, France, and Italy, almost every family had lost a son or close relative.[107]

---

[106] HISTORY OF WORLD WAR I, by General S.L.A. Marshall, American Heritage, NY 1982, p.232.

[107] A HISTORY OF WARFARE, by John Keegan, Vintage Books, Random House, NY, 1993, p.365.

Never before in history had Europe seen so much bloodshed in such a short period of time. This was the first "industrial war" in which the machines of mass production developed in factories had been adapted for mass destruction on the battlefield. It is why, until World War II, the First World War was called **The Great War.**

Through it all, the neutral Swiss, living peacefully in the center of the chaos, kept their rifles ready and watched the massacres, shaking their heads as they had so many times before.

Chris, the glory of war is the tenth deadly idea.

Uncle Eric

P.S. Nothing I am saying here should be taken as a criticism of machine guns or any other weapons. The world contains many powerseekers who would enslave or kill us if they had the chance. Guns help us hold these tyrants at bay.

Weapons are just tools, and like a hammer, knife, or chain saw, they can be used for good or evil. In World War I they were used for evil because there was no issue of right and wrong in that war, just groups of the Usual Suspects slugging it out, as they have for so many centuries.

Chris, you might argue that Archduke Franz Ferdinand had been murdered, so this justified action. But what kind of action?

It might have justified finding and punishing the individuals who killed him, but a world war?

Any time you hear "alliance," think "domino effect." Because of alliances, the death of one man led to the deaths of 15 million. The war had nothing to do with right and wrong, it was because of the simple promise, if one of us goes to war, we all will.

38

America's Entry Into World War I

Dear Chris,

Check encyclopedias or a library card catalog under the headings British Empire, Russian Empire, and French Empire. Then look for German Empire.

You will find mountains of information about the British, Russian, and French Empires, but little about a German Empire because there wasn't one.

Well, that is an overstatement. Berlin did capture a few territories, but its global "empire" was tiny compared to those of London, Moscow, and Paris.

After all, in 1914, Germany was a new country formed only 43 years earlier. German rulers were just getting started in their quest to subdue and annex other countries. The British, Russians, and French had been at it for centuries, killing and conquering millions all over the world.

Like Washington D.C. and Tokyo, Berlin could build its new empire only by stealing land and taxpayers from the governments who had conquered and stolen ahead of them.

So the British, French, and Russians regarded the Germans as aggressors.

Chris, these empires were the engine that spread the war throughout the Old World. As the Usual Suspects entered the war, they dragged their colonies in with them.

For instance, when the French entered the war, their colonies on the other side of the globe, called French

Indochina (now Vietnam, Laos, and Cambodia) suddenly found themselves at war with Germany and Austria. Most of the people in French Indochina had never even met a German or Austrian, but much to their surprise they were now at war with these people.

This was again the case in World War II. In my next series of letters about World War II, I will give you a lot more information about the British, French, and Russian Empires.

In World War I, the two sides, the Allies and Central Powers, were fairly evenly matched, and they quickly fought each other to a standstill. Territorial gains were made in other parts of the Old World, but along the most important front, between France and Germany, little of the battle line moved more than three miles during the entire course of the war.

This "Western Front" was a giant meat grinder into which young men were forced by the millions.

On Christmas in 1914 and 1915, a tiny glimmer of reason erupted. Troops from both sides left the trenches to sing carols and play soccer with the people they had been shooting at the day before.[108]

By spring of 1917, the troops began showing disturbing signs of rationality. Half the French combat divisions refused further orders to attack.[109] Russian units were in revolt, helping to overthrow their government. A peace movement had developed in Austria.

By late 1917, there was some danger that all soldiers on both sides would throw down their weapons and go home, ending the war.

---

[108] "Bertie Felstead," THE ECONOMIST, August 4, 2001, p.71.

[109] A HISTORY OF WARFARE, by John Keegan, Vintage Books, Random House, NY, 1993, p.361.

The troops' attitude toward the war can be seen from an anecdote told by British soldier A. Donovan Young. Young's unit was within sight of the enemy but found they could play soccer ("football") without being fired on. One day an officer decided that if they could play soccer in safety, they could practice their marching in safety. Marching was called company drill.

The officer commenced company drill when a shrapnel shell landed nearby, ending the exercise. The next day a patrol found a note pinned to a tree which said: "we like to watch you play football, and we shall not shell you while you play football, but we will shell you if we must watch you doing company drill."[110]

In the capitols of the Usual Suspects, there was panic. From the lips of every leader came the anguished cry, The war is dying! The war is dying! How will we save the war!?

Well, maybe this is an exaggeration, but not much. The last thing any powerseeker wants is to give a war and have no one show up for it.

To the rescue came America's President Woodrow Wilson, which brings us to the tremendously important "deadly idea" explained earlier — global protection.

When this horrific war erupted, President Wilson had declared that the U.S. would remain neutral. He urged all Americans to remain "impartial in thought as well as action."

But Britain was an island nation with a strong navy, and the British wanted to buy weapons and supplies from producers in the U.S.

---

[110] MILITARY ANECDOTES, edited by Max Hastings, Oxford University Press, NY 1985, p.369.

American producers were willing to sell to the British, so ships laden with American-made war goods began crossing the Atlantic.

The Germans had to stop these war goods from reaching the British, so they sent submarines to sink the ships. The most famous example was the luxury liner *Lusitania.* This liner was carrying 5,500 cases of ammunition to Britain,[111] as well as British and American passengers. The Germans knew about the ammunition, and the German Embassy in Washington D.C. publicly warned Americans not to travel on the ship.[112]

Americans took the risk anyhow, and on May 7, 1915, the *Lusitania* was torpedoed. Among the 1,198 lives lost were 124 Americans.

Nevertheless, American ships, cargoes, and passengers continued crossing to Britain, and more of them were sunk.

Chris, remember, the Barbary Wars set the precedent for global protection. The Spanish-American War gave Americans a taste for conquest.

Instead of President Wilson telling Americans, "When you go abroad you go at your own risk," he pledged to protect them no matter how risky the waters in which they chose to sail.

This was also an application of the deadly idea of cost externalization. Instead of the shippers providing their own armed escorts, the government did it for them using U.S. Navy ships. The costs and risks of supplying the British were shifted onto U.S. Navy sailors and U.S. taxpayers.

---

[111] "American Foreign Policy, The Turning Point," by Ralph Raico, THE FAILURE OF AMERICA'S FOREIGN WARS, edited by Richard Ebeling and Jacob Hornberger, The Future of Freedom Foundation, Fairfax, VA 1996, p.68.

[112] Grolier Encyclopedia CD-ROM under the subject, World War I.

Some officials in Wilson's government had long been sympathetic to the English and French, so, on April 6, 1917, just as World War I was in danger of going out of business, Congress, under Wilson's leadership, declared war against Germany.

President Wilson saved the war.

The Spanish-American War, the conquest of the Philippines, and the theft of Panama, had been great fun — the glory of war — so this new, much larger war would be even more fun, right?

Two million young American men were marched into the meat grinder singing the popular tune "Over There;" 116,000 did not come back.[113]

Incidentally, Chris, the vote to go to war was not unanimous. In the Senate it was 82-6, and in the House, 373-50.

One of the no votes was by Representative Jeannette Rankin who was the first woman ever elected to Congress. Rankin had taken office just four days before the vote. When asked why she voted against entering the war, she said "I knew that ...none of the idealistic hopes would be carried out, and I was aware of the falseness of much of the propaganda."[114] In 1941, Rankin would be the only member of either house to vote against entering World War II. I will write more about her when we come to that war.

The two million Americans with fine, modern weapons ended the stalemate. They tipped the balance in favor of the Allies and thereby infused new life into the war.

---

[113] World Almanac 2000, p.217.

[114] Votes for Women web site, www.huntington.org/vfw/imp/rankin.html

In every capitol — or at least the capitols of the Allies — the leaders breathed a sigh of relief. The war had been saved.

And through it all, the neutral Swiss, living peacefully in the center of the chaos, kept their rifles ready and watched the massacres, shaking their heads as they had so many times before.

Chris, let me emphasize that by 1917, this European and Asian war had one foot in the grave and the other on a banana peel.

The USG's entry saved the war, escalated it, and made it into mankind's first global war.

An often-overlooked point is that it was *just* a European and Asian war until the USG's entry. The USG's participation made it a genuine world war.

Another often overlooked point about this first global war is that the destruction of housing, clothing, waste disposal systems, and food supplies led to a decline in resistance to disease. In the final months of the war — after the USG's escalation —an epidemic of influenza broke out in the armies and spread around the world. This killed another 20 million, including a half-million Americans.[115] These 20 million are generally not included in estimates of the war's death toll. If they were, the toll would be 35 million, more than double what it was in April 1917 when Wilson saved the war.

Chris, we must never forget that like the 15 million killed directly in the war, every one of the 20 million dead from the epidemic was a living, breathing human being who was loved by someone.

---

[115] "Slouching Toward Catastrophe," by George H. Nash, IMPRIMIS NEWSLETTER, Hillsdale College, Hillsdale, MI, April 1992.

As I have said before, the country and the government are not the same thing. America is a wonderful country, I would not want to live anywhere else. But the U.S. Government, ignoring George Washington's advice to stay out of the wars of Europe,[116] continually meddles in other people's conflicts, making them worse.

How much worse? Shortly I will tell you about the Treaty of Versailles. You will be amazed.

But first, Chris, you might run up against people who think the philosophy of America's Founders is outdated. They believe that what happened in 1787 is no longer relevant to the world we live in today.

Always remember that America's Founders attempted to establish a government that would provide the most liberty and the greatest economic prosperity. They studied world history and political philosophy to determine what worked in the past — and what did not. The result was the government they put in place in 1787. A central principle of this government was international neutrality — never get involved with the governments of Europe because they are, in Jefferson's words, "nations of eternal war."

In the broad scheme of things, the United States has a very brief history. Put another way, do you remember the LITTLE HOUSE® BOOKS[117] written by Laura Ingalls Wilder? A television series, LITTLE HOUSE ON THE PRAIRIE starring Michael

---

[116] See GEORGE WASHINGTON'S FAREWELL ADDRESS which was delivered on September 17, 1796. Available through Bluestocking Press, web site: www.BluestockingPress.com).

[117] THE LITTLE HOUSE® BOOKS by Laura Ingalls Wilder., HarperTrophy® Publishers, New York, circa 1935. Dates are taken from the LAURA INGALLS WILDER AND ROSE WILDER LANE TIMETABLE, compiled by Jane A. Williams, published by Bluestocking Press, web site: www.BluestockingPress.com

Landon was loosely based on the books. Consider this. Pa Ingalls, Laura's father, was born the same year James Madison and Betsy Ross died. Laura died the same year that Sputnik was placed into orbit.

So we are not too many generations removed from the original American Founders. Ask yourself, how far removed are we from America's founding principles?

Uncle Eric

P.S. Chris, a British soldier once explained why he could mingle with enemy soldiers, even shake hands and exchange Christmas gifts with them, and the next day go back to killing them. It gives much insight about the Old World, and why America's Founders advised us never to get involved in their wars. The British soldier said, "[My battalion] never allowed itself to have any political feelings about the Germans. A professional soldier's duty was simply to fight whomever the King ordered him to fight."[118]

In the conquest of the Philippines, this European attitude was enthusiastically embraced by the American armed forces, and it remains so today.

---

[118] "Bertie Felstead," THE ECONOMIST, August 4, 2001, p.71.

39

The Third Choice Ignored

Dear Chris,

The first casualty of war is truth. To justify America's entry into World War I, the USG launched a blizzard of propaganda describing Germany as an evil monster that was trying to take over the world. The government hired an army of 75,000 speakers[119] to tour the country painting all Germans as bloodthirsty, satanic brutes. Much of this message would be repeated 25 years later in the film series WHY WE FIGHT.

Anyone who advocated staying out of World War I was branded an isolationist. The Espionage Act of June 15, 1917, and the Sedition Act of May 16, 1918, made "disloyal speech" illegal.[120]

In AMERICA IN THE GREAT WAR, Ronald Schaffer's first chapter, "Managing American Minds," describes two of the government's propaganda posters titled "Destroy this Mad Brute," and "The **Hohenzollern** [121] Dream." Chris, as you read Schaffer's descriptions, bear in mind that the Allies —

---

[119] "World War I and the Great Departure," by Wesley Allen Riddle, THE FAILURE OF AMERICA'S FOREIGN WARS, edited by Richard Ebeling and Jacob Hornberger, The Future of Freedom Foundation, Fairfax, VA 1996, p.82.

[120] "World War I and the Great Departure," by Wesley Allen Riddle, THE FAILURE OF AMERICA'S FOREIGN WARS, edited by Richard Ebeling and Jacob Hornberger, The Future of Freedom Foundation, Fairfax, VA 1996, p.83.

[121] Hohenzollern: the ruling family of Prussia and Germany.

the British, French, and Russians — had been around for centuries and had already attacked and conquered about a third of the world. Little Germany was just getting started. Writes Schaffer:

> Some of the more lurid posters added fantasies about enemy attacks on the United States. In "Destroy this Mad Brute," a monstrous wild-eyed ape with a Kaiser Wilhelm mustache and huge drops of saliva dripping from its gaping mouth stands on a piece of land labeled "AMERICA." It carries with its left arm (which has matted fur and blood on it) a light-skinned woman whose long gray dress has been torn down, leaving her breasts exposed. The woman covers her face with one hand while holding the side of her head with the other. The ape wields a club labeled "**KULTUR**"[122] and its spiked helmet is inscribed with the word "MILITARISM." "The Hohenzollern Dream" depicts a gigantic, portly German soldier, also with a Kaiser Wilhelm mustache, holding a rifle and bayonet on one shoulder while a vulture perches on the other. His left boot is partly immersed in New York harbor, and with his right boot he is crushing the towers of skyscrapers.[123]

Chris, look at a globe. Compare the U.S. to Germany. The idea that little Germany had enough troops, ships, and

---

[122] Kultur: (pronounced cool-tour) German culture and civilization. Used in U.S. propaganda to mean the German mind, the thinking of all Germans.

[123] AMERICA IN THE GREAT WAR, by Ronald Schaffer, Oxford University Press, NY, 1991, p.9.

guns to cross the Atlantic and conquer the U.S., the most powerful industrial giant in history, was entirely crazy, but Americans had war fever and were not interested in facts.

German books were burned outside numerous libraries, and the music of German composer Beethoven was banned from symphonies.[124]

Sauerkraut, a German dish, was renamed "liberty cabbage."

German-Americans named Schmitz changed their names to Smith, and almost every German street and landmark was renamed.

In 1918 in St. Louis, a German-American was bound in an American flag and lynched by a mob.[125]

The assumption was that there were only two possible foreign policies. One was for America to cut itself off entirely from the rest of the world. The other was to be, using the modern term, "engaged" in the world, which in actual practice means getting into other people's wars.

A middle ground was not considered. The idea of private citizens and companies visiting other nations, doing business with them, and being friends with them — and taking all the risks — and the government having no connections, was not part of the debate. The two choices were: isolationism or engagement.

---

[124] "World War I and the Great Departure," by Wesley Allen Riddle, THE FAILURE OF AMERICA'S FOREIGN WARS, edited by Richard Ebeling and Jacob Hornberger, The Future of Freedom Foundation, Fairfax, VA 1996, p.83.

[125] "World War I and the Great Departure," by Wesley Allen Riddle, THE FAILURE OF AMERICA'S FOREIGN WARS, edited by Richard Ebeling and Jacob Hornberger, The Future of Freedom Foundation, Fairfax, VA 1996, p.83.

Those who favored engagement won because they perceived only one other choice, isolationism, which meant cutting America totally off from the rest of the world. Americans (rightfully) perceived isolationism as an impossible option because Americans needed to communicate with others and to buy raw materials and other goods from them. They couldn't understand George Washington's alternative, neutrality: trade with them, visit with them, but no political ties, and, especially, don't get involved in their wars.

This forced choice between only two alternatives was so effectively created in World War I that it remains solidly entrenched in the American mind today. It is what the USG's foreign policy has been built on during my entire lifetime.

And the image of Germans as bloodthirsty brutes trying to invade and conquer America, and ravage American women, carried through to World War II, greasing the skids for America's entry into that war.

With mighty America engaged in the First World War, the stalemate ended. The scales were tipped steeply in favor of the Allies and against the Central Powers.

On November 11, 1918, the severely beaten Germans surrendered, and the other Central Powers followed shortly thereafter.

Fifteen miles from the Austrian border, near the little town of Traunstein, was a prison camp for captured Russians. One of the guards, a corporal, was shivering in the deep snow when news of the surrender arrived. We do not know what the young corporal was thinking, but we can be sure he was not happy. His name was Adolph Hitler.

After the surrender, the Allies, which now included the USG, forced a peace treaty onto the Germans at the Palace of Versailles in France. That treaty was one of the greatest mistakes in all of world history; it was the beginning of Hitler's career.

Uncle Eric

P.S. Chris, if you haven't already read the book EXTRAORDINARY POPULAR DELUSIONS AND THE MADNESS OF CROWDS[126] now might be a good time. Whenever you feel as if you are being drawn into a crowd mentality, ask yourself if you are using logic and reason to form your opinions, or sheer emotion.

Again, as Senator Hiram Johnson warned in 1917, "The first casualty when war comes is truth."

---

[126] EXTRAORDINARY POPULAR DELUSIONS AND THE MADNESS OF CROWDS by Charles Mackay, published by Crown Publishers, New York, 1980.

40

They Will Fight Over Anything

Dear Chris,

Before we get into the Treaty of Versailles, let me point out something very important but often overlooked.

I challenge you to find one acre of ground anywhere in the Old World that has not been fought over at one time or another.

As I write this, the governments of India and Pakistan are fighting over ownership of a glacier. I kid you not.

Glaciers are the most worthless real estate on earth. These unstable rivers of ice are too dangerous to have any use. They contain hidden crevasses that can swallow a person forever.

The 46-mile long Siachen Glacier is in the Karakoram Mountains in the Himalaya region. Military camps are at 18,000 feet and some forward positions are at 21,000, more than a mile higher than the Rockies. A soldier who is not wearing an oxygen mask can run only about 50 paces before he passes out.

If Old World governments will shed blood over a glacier, they will do it for anything.

That is what the Old World has been like since Cain killed Abel. Tens of millions have been slaughtered for reasons that rational persons can only shake their heads at.

For two centuries, pundits have claimed that the Old World governments have become enlightened and war will fade away. Usually their arguments have been hard to hear due to the roar of the cannons.

> As Donald Kagan dryly notes, "Over the past two centuries the only thing more common than predictions about the end of war has been war itself."
> ... In 1968, Will and Ariel Durant calculated that only 268 of the previous 3,421 years had been free of war. And no year has been since 1968.
>
> — George Will
> WASHINGTON POST, July 16, 1995

Nearly all the wars have been in the Old World. And Old World governments instigated most of the worst of the ones in the New World. Examples are the Spanish conquests of the Aztecs and Incas.

Chris, my point is this. Until the U.S. Government got into them, neither of the World Wars was unusual except in the number of people killed (due to the new technologies). This behavior was the same thing the governments of the Old World had been doing for thousands of years.

What made these wars into "world" wars was the U.S. getting involved in them. Up to that point, they had been confined to Europe, Asia, and Africa.

Uncle Eric

41

The Treaty of Versailles

Dear Chris,

The U.S. Government and Hollywood tend to see things in terms of good guys versus bad guys. For example, In World War II the Axis powers, led by Germany, were the bad guys; Britain, France, and the other Allied powers were the good guys. In World War I, same thing; the Allies were the good guys and the Central Powers, led by Germany, were the bad guys.

We are led to believe that in the Second World War, Germans were swept away by Hitler's charismatic blood lust.

However, all nations at all times have a depressingly large supply of crazy power junkies, and they do not follow them into World Wars. Or, at least, they do not follow them with the enthusiasm that millions of Germans followed Hitler. Why did the Germans do this?

The mystery deepens when we realize that one solution to the power junkie problem is to have a population intelligent enough to recognize a powerseeker and ignore him. On this score Germany was way ahead of nearly all other countries. It was one of the most advanced and educated nations in the world, a leader in science and the arts.

Yet, in 1937, when Hitler announced his plan to grab more *lebensraum* (living space), Germans cheered. Why did these intelligent people respond to Hitler's call?

Queen Mary

Carthaginian

Chris, visit the town of Lahina in Hawaii and you will see
the answer. In a previous set of letters[127] I wrote:

> Docked at Lahina on the island of Maui is a small
> sailing ship called the *Carthaginian*. This two-masted
> brig appears to be from the 1700s but it was built in
> Germany after World War I when the rest of Europe
> was in the era of giant steamships like the *Queen Mary*.
> In the attempt to keep the Germans subservient, British
> and French rulers had restricted their capacity to
> rebuild their economy. Germans were allowed to
> manufacture ships no longer than 100 feet with no
> more than 35 horsepower — that of a motorcycle
> engine. The Queen Mary was 1,020 feet and over
> 100,000 horsepower. Germans had no choice but to
> revert to wind power.

It gets worse. At the end of World War I, Allied rulers
forced the Germans to accept the Treaty of Versailles,
including Articles 231 and 232. The treaty was presented to
the German people on May 7, 1919.

Article 231 said the Germans and their partners alone,
not the British, French, or any of the other Allied powers,
were responsible for the war. Article 232 said the Germans
should pay for it.

> Article 231: The Allied and Associated Governments
> affirm and Germany accepts the responsibility of

---

[127] Uncle Eric is referring to the book THE THOUSAND YEAR WAR IN THE
MIDEAST: HOW IT AFFECTS YOU TODAY by Richard J. Maybury, published by
Bluestocking Press, web site: www.BluestockingPress.com

Germany and her allies for causing all the loss and damage to which the Allied and Associated Governments and their nationals have been subjected as a consequence of the war imposed upon them by the aggression of Germany and her allies.

Article 232 (in part): The Allied and Associated Governments, however, require, and Germany undertakes, that she will make compensation for all damage done to the civilian population of the Allied and Associated Powers and to their property during the period of the belligerency of each as an Allied or Associated Power against Germany by such aggression by land, by sea and from the air, and in general all damage as defined in Annex 1 hereto.

The "innocent" British, French, and their allies collected reparations from the Germans. These included but were not limited to:

• Alsace and Lorraine, given to France

• Lands around the towns of Eupen and Malmedy, given to Belgium

• 132 million gold marks[128]

• factory machines

• 75% of Germany's iron ore deposits

---

[128] = 1.5 million ounces of gold.

- 200,000 telephone and telegraph poles

- 5,000 railroad engines

- 150,000 railroad cars

- 5,000 trucks

- 72% of Germany's zinc deposits

- 57% of Germany's lead deposits

- 75% of Germany's iron industry

- 20% of Germany's coal industry

- All of Germany's overseas colonies

- All of Germany's overseas financial assets

  Also, according to the Treaty of Versailles:

- Germany's Saarland was given to the League of Nations, and the Saarland's coal production was to go to France for 15 years.

- The German navy was abolished.

- The German army was disbanded except for 100,000 troops.

- No German troops were allowed on German land west of the Rhine River.

- The newly created nation of Poland was given the German territories of West Prussia and Posen.

- The port of Danzig, an ancient German city, was taken away and given to the League of Nations.

In other words, Chris, Allied rulers placed the entire blame for the First World War, not just on the German government, but on the German people, too. They stole vast amounts of the German people's property and tried to crush the Germans to force them back into the poverty of a pre-industrial society.

One of my uncles was an American veteran of World War II. He did not understand what the war was about until long after it was over. His summary was, "The Allies got the Germans down on the ground with their boots on their necks and would not let them up."

When the Treaty of Versailles was being drafted, the famous economist John Maynard Keynes quit the conference in protest. He returned home and wrote THE ECONOMIC CONSEQUENCES OF THE PEACE in which he predicted that the Treaty of Versailles would so impoverish the Germans that it would lead to another great war.

The French General Ferdinand Foch warned, "This is not peace, but a truce for 20 years." That was an amazingly accurate prediction. Hitler's invasion of Poland came in 1939, twenty years after the Treaty of Versailles.

Remember Bismark's comment, "A generation that has taken a beating is always followed by a generation that deals one."

Chris, abuse of the Germans did not end with the reparations. In 1923, the French government reported that the Germans were not making their payments on time. French soldiers were sent to invade and occupy the Ruhr Valley, which was Germany's industrial heartland. This unified the Germans as they had not been since before the war.[129]

So, Chris, here is a summary, the essential chain of events in World War I that led to World War II:

- Under the deadly idea of global protection for U.S. shipping, the USG entered the war.

- America's fresh troops and weapons destroyed the stalemate and tipped the scales heavily in favor of Britain, France, and the other Allies.

- The Allies smashed the German armed forces, then forced the Treaty of Versailles onto the German government and the German people.

- The treaty put all the blame for the war on the Germans, made them pay for the damage, and thereby made them destitute and desperate.

The Great Depression of the 1930s added to the Germans' desperation until they were ready to fly into the arms of anyone who would promise to make them strong and prosperous again. Anyone.

Chris, here is something to think about:

America should have minded her own business and stayed out of the World War [the First World War]. If you hadn't entered the war the Allies would have

---

[129] PRELUDE TO WAR, Time-Life Books, Alexandria, VA 1976, p.89.

made peace with Germany in the spring of 1917. Had we made peace then there would have been no collapse in Russia followed by Communism, and Germany would not have signed the Versailles Treaty, which has enthroned Nazism in Germany. If America had stayed out of the war, all these 'isms' wouldn't today be sweeping the continent in Europe and breaking down parliamentary government, and if England had made peace early in 1917, it would have saved over one million British, French, and American and other lives.

Those are the words of Winston Churchill in an August 1936 interview in the NEW YORK ENQUIRER newspaper. Churchill is a legend, Britain's leader in World War II.

Let me be very clear about this, Chris. World War II was the worst thing humans have ever done, and the U.S. Government's meddling in World War I was the chief cause of it.

Until the U.S. entry into the First World War, the Central Powers were fairly evenly matched against the Allies. This is why the Western Front was a huge stalemate.

The U.S. presence made the Allies overwhelmingly powerful, which enabled the British and French to force the harsh terms of the Versailles Treaty onto the Germans.

Chris, in my opinion, every one of the tens of millions killed in World War II should have been buried in Washington D.C., and each tombstone should have been given the inscription "Made in the U.S.A" as a reminder of what can happen when Americans get involved in the politics of the Old World.

But you haven't heard the worst of it. The USG's meddling in World War I was a horrific mistake, but its meddling in World War II was vastly worse. I will cover that war in my next set of letters.[130]

Uncle Eric

---

[130] Uncle Eric is referring to Richard J. Maybury's book WORLD WAR II: THE REST OF THE STORY, part two in Maybury's World War series, published by Bluestocking Press, web site: www.BluestockingPress.com

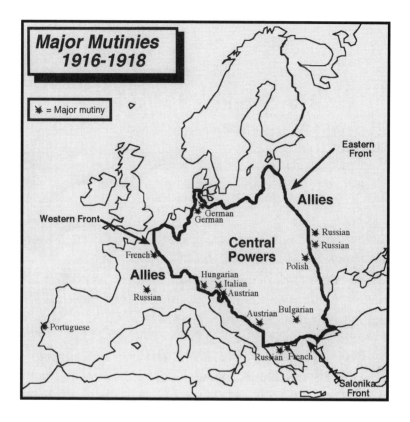

Major Mutinies 1916-1918

✴ = Major mutiny

Eastern Front

Western Front

German
German

Allies

French

Central Powers

✴ Russian
✴ Russian
✴
Polish

Hungarian
✴ ✴ Italian
✴ Austrian

Allies

✴
Russian

Austrian Bulgarian
✴

✴ Portuguese

Russian French

Salonika Front

By 1916, the two sides had fought each other to a standstill. Then the fronts barely moved for two years. The terrible conditions of trench warfare and the troops' realization that they were dying for nothing, led to rebellion and the danger that the war would end. In addition to the major mutinies shown here, there were thousands of acts of individual rebellion in all European armies. By 1917, the war was in danger of going out of business. Then the U.S. Government got into it.

Source: ATLAS OF THE FIRST WORLD WAR by Martin Gilbert
Oxford University Press, NY, 1994, p.137

42

The Sound of Reloading

Dear Chris,

Remember Bismark's comment: "A generation that has taken a beating is always followed by a generation that deals one."[131]

The Treaty of Versailles was the end of World War I and the beginning of World War II.

Another way to look at it is that the First World War did not end until 1945, and this was the fault of the USG for getting into it in 1917 and imposing the brutal Treaty of Versailles on the German people.

The Allies' propaganda against the Germans had been so effective that the hatred continued after World War I and along with it the British blockade of food supplies. For six months after they had laid down their arms, the Germans watched their children die of starvation. The British blockade eventually murdered an estimated 800,000 Germans.[132]

The British did it because they could; they were backed by the mighty USG.

---

[131] HISTORY OF WORLD WAR I, by General S.L.A. Marshall, American Heritage, NY 1982, p.22.

[132] "The Roots of World War II," by Sheldon Richman, THE FAILURE OF AMERICA'S FOREIGN WARS, edited by Richard Ebeling and Jacob Hornberger, The Future of Freedom Foundation, Fairfax, VA 1996, p.91.

So the quiet the world heard during the two decades between the World Wars was not the sound of peace, it was the sound of people reloading.

One of the many weak points in the Treaty of Versailles was Article 8 and other parts that required Germany's disarmament to be the beginning of global disarmament.

The Germans did disarm because they were beaten into submission and had no choice.

After their disarmament, the Germans said to the other powers, now that we have kept our side of the deal, you must keep yours.

When Hitler made an offer to destroy the last German machine gun if the British and French would do the same, the British and French backed out. Their breaking of the agreement was a legal release of Germany from its obligation, and the Germans began to rearm.[133]

The British had the world's largest navy, and the French built the most elaborate fortification in history, the Maginot Line, along their eastern border.

History repeats. Governments keep making the same mistakes because they cling to the same ideas they have had since the days of the Roman Empire. The military buildups that preceded the First World War, and so many wars before that, were happening again.

Uncle Eric

---

[133] THE ORIGINS OF WORLD WAR II, by Alfred von Wegerer, Richard R. Smith Publishing, New York, 1941, p.16.

43

Hitler's Rise

Dear Chris,

Hitler got his start during the German hyperinflation. The German government had no way to pay all the penalties levied by the Treaty of Versailles, so it began to print money. As the number of marks increased, the value of each individual mark fell, and prices rose to compensate.

The German hyperinflation of the early 1920s was one of the worst in all of world history. When the war ended in 1918, a pound of butter cost 3.0 marks. Five years later the price hit 6,000,000,000,000 (six trillion) marks.

The value of the German people's savings was wiped out. In effect, their savings had been confiscated by their government and sent to the Allies. (Chris, if you need a refresher on hyperinflation, you might want to review my previous sets of letters.[134])

This, on top of the Versailles reparations, meant that by 1924, millions of Germans who had been middle class or wealthy before the war were living in poverty, wondering where their next meal would come from.

---

[134] Uncle Eric is referring to WHATEVER HAPPENED TO PENNY CANDY, as well as THE MONEY MYSTERY, both written by Richard J. Maybury and published by Bluestocking Press, web site: www.BluestockingPress.com

The Germans knew who was responsible for their suffering, the Allies, and they would not forget.

This horrific effect of the Versailles Treaty was fully understood in the U.S. Capitol. President Wilson did everything he could to persuade Americans to accept the treaty because it contained the seeds of the **League of Nations**,[135] but he failed; when he submitted the treaty to the Senate in 1919, the Senate voted it down.

But Wilson and his successor Warren G. Harding continued as allies of the British and French, so the Germans did not have a prayer of resisting the treaty.

Chris, remember the corporal who was standing guard the night that Germany surrendered? In July, 1921, as the hyperinflation was fast accelerating, that corporal, Adolph Hitler, became leader of a small group of angry Germans called the National Socialist German Worker's Party — the Nazi Party. Nazism was a form of fascism.

By 1923, the hyperinflation was raging, and radical political parties were springing up all over Germany. Hitler's Nazis tried to forcibly take over the government of the German state of Bavaria.

They failed, and Hitler went to prison where he wrote MEIN KAMPF, which means My Battle. Regarded as the handbook of Nazism, MEIN KAMPF explains Hitler's ideas on

---

[135] League of Nations: predecessor of the United Nations; the first attempt to create a world government. The failure of the League of Nations to stop Italy's invasion of Ethiopia is often cited as a cause of World War II. Many Americans bemoan the loss of the League and the incompetence of the United Nations because they believe a single world government that can force its will onto anyone, anywhere is the way to create peace and liberty for all.

anti-Semitism, anti-Communism, superiority of the so-called **Aryan race**,[136] German **nationalism** and the state's superiority over the individual.

In America, anyone who was not blinded by the bigotry created by the war's propaganda could see that the impoverishment of the Germans was leading to another war. Germans were in the U.S. trying to borrow money to pay the reparations and replace what the Allies had stolen from them. In a misguided attempt to help them, the U.S. Federal Reserve expanded the money supply and much of the new money went to Germany.[137] In THE RISE AND FALL OF THE THIRD REICH, William L. Shirer explains that Germany had become dependent on loans from foreigners,

> ...America above all, from whose swollen coffers loans were pouring in to make and keep Germany prosperous. Between 1924 and 1930 German borrowing amounted to some seven billion dollars and most of it came from American investors, who gave little thought to how the Germans might make eventual payment. The Germans gave even less thought to it.[138]

Much of the money newly created by the Federal Reserve also went into the U.S. stock market, creating a huge speculative bubble.

---

[136] Aryan race: a Nazi propaganda term meaning a Nordic Caucasian of non-Jewish descent.

[137] AMERICA'S GREAT DEPRESSION by Murray Rothbard, Richard and Snyder Publishing, NY 1983, p.121-122.

[138] THE RISE AND FALL OF THE THIRD REICH, by William L. Shirer, Simon and Schuster, NY 1960, p.117.

In 1929, the Federal Reserve halted its inflation of the money supply, the bubble burst, and a depression began. In a domino effect, the depression spread around the world. The Usual Suspects, still deeply hateful toward each other, levied tit-for-tat trade restrictions on each other. The restrictions reduced everyone's ability to buy and sell. Businesses went broke and millions lost their jobs. The depression turned into the global Great Depression.

On top of all the other trouble from the depression, and from the hyperinflation of the 1920s, and from the reparations, the Germans were unable to repay their loans.

Chris, weakened Germany was hit harder by the depression than any other major nation.

You have read stories about Americans losing their homes and businesses. You have seen photographs and films of hungry Americans standing in bread lines.

Whatever you have seen, in Germany it was worse.

Shirer writes, "the factories were silent, when the registered unemployed numbered over six million and bread lines stretched for blocks in every city in the land."[139]

For the Germans this was the last straw. Already paranoid from the way they were abused after the last war, the hungry Germans went completely around the bend. Not all of them, certainly, but enough.

Actually, to my mind, it is amazing that the Germans did not go crazier than they did. Imagine if America had been smashed, robbed, and pounded into the dirt as the Germans had been; how do you think Americans would react?

Uncle Eric

---

[139] THE RISE AND FALL OF THE THIRD REICH, by William L. Shirer, Simon and Schuster, NY 1960, p.136.

44

U.S. Invades Russia

Dear Chris,

Before we look more closely at events in Germany after World War I, we need to look at Russia.

One of the most important events of the 20th century remains almost unknown in America. You can test this yourself. Ask anyone you know: Has the U.S. ever invaded Russia?

The answer is yes. In 1918, the USG and its allies invaded Russia, and that invasion still haunts us today. Here is the story.

For centuries until World War I, Russians had lived under the tyranny of the Czars. (Czar means Caesar.)

Rebellions and assassinations became Russia's national sports. The first four years of the reign of Czar Nicholas I, for instance, in 1825-29, saw 41 peasant uprisings. The army, especially the **Cossacks**,[140] were continually riding from one end of Russia to the other to put down these rebellions.

Generally the army was successful, the peasants were poorly armed — pitchforks and shovels against rifles.

Then came the First World War. This conflict was so huge that millions of Russians were sent to fight against the Germans.

---

[140] Cossacks: an ethnic group located mostly in Southern Russia. Militantly Christian, Cossacks were "the sword arm of the Czars" against the Turks (Muslims), and against anyone who rebelled against the Czars.

For the first time, millions of Russians held modern weapons in their hands. Imagine what it felt like, Chris, the difference between a pitchfork and a machine gun.

The peasants decided they would rather use these weapons against the Czar than against the German Kaiser (Kaiser also means Caesar). The Czar was overthrown and killed. This was the 1917 Russian Revolution. (Chris, for a taste of what it was like to be an ordinary Russian caught in the turmoil of the Russian Revolution, watch the movie DR. ZHIVAGO.)

Disagreeing about who should be the Russian government, Russians splintered into dozens of **factions**.

By 1918, the faction that appeared to be coming out on top in this free-for-all was a group of socialists known as the Bolsheviks, or the Reds.

In other parts of the world, including the U.S., socialism was not yet as popular as it would be in later decades, and several governments decided they should stop the Reds from coming to power in Russia.

However, they did not have a plan beyond that. They knew who they did not want running the Russian government, but they did not know who they did want.

This was very similar to the situation the USG and its allies faced following the invasion of Afghanistan, Iraq, and other parts of the Islamic world because of the September 11th attacks. They knew who they did not want in power, but they did not know who they did want. The Old World is not exactly overflowing with Thomas Jeffersons and James Madisons. In most cases, the few leaders who do show some interest in real liberty are quickly killed off by the legions of powerseekers in their own countries.

In 1918, U.S officials decided to invade Russia anyhow, under the deadly idea of protecting "interests."

Washington, Tokyo, London, Prague, Paris, and Rome all sent troops to invade Russia and conquer the Reds.

There is reason to believe that some of these governments, especially Tokyo, also wanted to capture Russian land. In Washington, officials did not know what orders to give the troops, so orders were vague and confused. They amounted to, do whatever appears necessary. No one was quite sure what necessary meant.

The troops ended up marching aimlessly around the frozen Russian landscape, occasionally fighting with whoever tried to stop them, but accomplishing nothing.

Sergeant Silver Parish described one encounter: "We were ordered to burn a small village where the enemy could do effective sniping. Women opened fire on us, and we had to advance without firing upon them. We took 14 enemy prisoners and killed two. Then we burned the village. My heart ached to have the women fall down at my feet and grab my legs and kiss my hand and beg me not to do it. But orders are orders."[141]

The invasion failed, and the troops were withdrawn in 1920 after 200 Americans had been killed.

Chris, you can read about the American invasion of Russia in Chapter 18 of THE DECISION TO INTERVENE by historian George F. Kennan.[142]

Kennan reports that, at one point, 24 different governments had been set up in Russia, and the U.S. troops had no idea which they were supposed to help and which they were supposed to fight. He writes that President Wilson "did prevent them [the troops] from having any proper understanding of the purposes for which they were being used."

Most importantly, Kennan points out, Wilson, "rendered the United States vulnerable to the charge, which Soviet

---

[141] U.S. NEWS & WORLD REPORT, November 11, 1996, p.53.

[142] THE DECISION TO INTERVENE, by George F. Kennan, W.W. Norton & Co., NY, 1956.

propagandists have never ceased to exploit, of interfering by armed force" in Russia.

Few Americans have ever been taught about the U.S. invasion of Russia, so during the Cold War, which began in 1945, each time Russian leaders told their people the U.S. might invade, Americans laughed. If you had stopped a thousand Americans on the street and asked them, is it realistic for Russians to fear that America might attack them, I am sure 999 would have said, certainly not. But the Russians knew the U.S. had already invaded their homeland in 1918, so they supported the Kremlin, which was their only shield against the U.S., and they have never trusted us.

Chris, the horrific results remain with us today. More than eight decades after that invasion, thousands of Russian missiles stand ready to destroy America, and thousands of American missiles stand ready to destroy Russia.

We can be sure that none of the American troops slogging through the snows of Siberia in 1918 had any idea that they were helping create a situation that could someday destroy the world. The invention of guided missiles and nuclear bombs was still a quarter-century away.

Chris, you never know where actions will lead when someone violates the fundamental law that says, do not encroach on other persons or their property.[143] In the Spanish-American War, violating that law became the official policy of the USG. Awash in war fever, few Americans opposed this policy. The invasion of Russia, which then led to the Cold War and the threat of nuclear annihilation, are two of the many disasters it has produced.

Uncle Eric

---

[143] The two fundamental laws are thoroughly discussed in Richard J. Maybury's book WHATEVER HAPPENED TO JUSTICE? published by Bluestocking Press, web site: www.BluestockingPress.com

45

Desperation and the Neutrality Act

Dear Chris,

Now, I'll get back to Germany.

It is very important that you understand how the Germans felt. Close your eyes and picture in your mind everyone you love — your mother, father, grandparents, uncles, aunts, friends, everyone.

Imagine them jobless and desperately hungry. They have lost so much weight that their clothing hangs loosely on them, and they are in serious danger of starving to death. Several are ill due to lowered resistance to disease.

People in neighboring countries have done this to those you love — you know this. These people are making your dear family and friends pay for a war in which their own governments were as guilty as yours.

Chris, how would you feel? What would you do?

This is not to justify anything the Germans (or anyone else) did in World War II. It is only to say that the German people did not go crazy because they were evil or because of their so-called Prussian heritage. They went crazy because the Allies drove them to it.

Everyone has a breaking point.

In the poverty of the depression, Hitler's poisonous ideas found fertile soil. He promised to make Germany strong and prosperous again and to vanquish its enemies. Hitler gave the desperate, angry Germans hope, so his popularity grew.

In the March 1933 elections, the Nazi party got 43 percent of the vote. No other party was so popular, so the Nazis took control of the government. In the same month, the first concentration camp was erected at Dachau.

In August 1934, Hitler proclaimed himself Fuhrer (leader).

He set up a so-called command economy in which government agencies ordered businesses and individuals to do whatever the agencies believed necessary. Under these orders, businesses hired workers, and unemployment fell.

What were the businesses and workers producing?

Weapons.

Chris, in March 1935, Hitler introduced conscription to rebuild the army, navy, and air force. This military buildup violated the Treaty of Versailles.

The next month, the governments of Britain and France protested this violation.

Hitler ignored them. His intentions had been declared eleven years earlier in MEIN KAMPF. Now he was creating the armed forces to carry out those intentions.

The coming war was now obvious to anyone who knew Europe's history.

That same month enough Americans became so worried that Congress passed the Neutrality Act which required: 1) that the USG stay out of the Old World's wars, and 2) that the USG offer no assistance to governments in these wars.

Congress remembered how America had gotten into World War I, so in the Neutrality Act, it ordered the President to give no protection to U.S. citizens who take the risk of entering a war zone.[144]

---

[144] WORLD WAR II DAY BY DAY by Donald Sommerville, Dorset Press, Greenwich, CT, 1989, p.11.

Chris, as you know, the Neutrality Act did not work; the U.S. entered the new war anyhow. In my next set of letters[145] I will give you the rest of the story about World War II — the part you are not likely to get anywhere else.

Uncle Eric

P.S. Chris, I hope you took the time to examine the footnotes in this set of letters. As I said early on, you will find the research is not from esoteric sources that you cannot check. It's from material that has been freely available to the general public and to historians for years.

All I have done is rearrange and highlight the facts according to the two laws explained in my previous set of letters on law[146]— especially, Do not encroach on other persons or their property. This causes the facts to paint a picture much different than the one commonly accepted.

---

[145] Uncle Eric is referring to Richard J. Maybury's book WORLD WAR II: THE REST OF THE STORY, part two in Maybury's World War series, published by Bluestocking Press, web site: www.BluestockingPress.com

[146] Uncle Eric is referring to Richard J. Maybury's book WHATEVER HAPPENED TO JUSTICE?, published by Bluestocking Press, web site: www.BluestockingPress.com

46

Summary

Dear Chris,

I will end this set of letters about World War I and the ideas and events leading to it with a summary. Then we will go on to the next set of letters about World War II.[147]

The Hollywood view of the World Wars, launched by the movie series WHY WE FIGHT, is not truth. It is not even a half-truth. It is a deception.

Neither World War was a straightforward battle between good guys and bad guys. Both were much more complicated, and good versus evil had little to do with either of them.

Mostly they were just Old World governments behaving as Old World governments have always behaved. You can see this from this set of letters about World War I. In my next set you will see the same thing about World War II. That is the way the Old World has always been, and still is.

A fundamental belief of the American Founders was that political power corrupts the morals and the judgment. No one can be trusted with it, so the U.S. Government must be kept very limited. In foreign affairs, America must stay neutral, and our main system of defense must be the one

---

[147] Uncle Eric is referring to Richard J. Maybury's book WORLD WAR II: THE REST OF THE STORY, part two in Maybury's World War series, published by Bluestocking Press, web site: www.BluestockingPress.com

described in the Second Amendment (and used so effectively by the Swiss for centuries).

Chris, I have never seen any evidence to contradict the belief that political power corrupts, and I have seen a mountain of evidence to confirm it. Probably the most dramatic example is that the USG's participation in World War I produced the Treaty of Versailles, which led to World War II. In all of world history, I know of no greater mistake in morals or judgment.

Another key point to remember from this set of letters is that humans have inflicted more than 14,000 wars on themselves,[148] and the vast majority have been in the Old World. All of the worst wars of the twentieth century were in the Old World.

Both World Wars were typical, garden-variety European and Asian bloodbaths until the USG got into them. It was the USG's participation that turned them into World Wars. And this participation did not suddenly spring from nothing. I believe it was the logical result of ten deadly ideas that lead to war:

- **The Pax Romana.** This is the belief in the need to recreate the "Roman Peace," which, in actual fact, never existed. A key feature is belief in the need for a strong central government that dominates everyone. The desire for a new Pax Romana has been strong in Europe since the Middle Ages, and it remains strong today.

---

[148] DIRTY LITTLE SECRETS, by James F. Dunnigan and Albert A. Nofi, Quill/William Morrow, 1990, p.419.

- **Fascism.** A complement to the Pax Romana, fascism is the original Roman philosophy. It says that everyone should be "unified" under a single government that does whatever it believes necessary, no limits.

- **Love of Political Power.** Political power is the legal privilege of using force on persons who have not harmed anyone. This is the privilege that sets government apart from all other institutions, and it is the privilege sought by political powerseekers. War is the most exciting use of political power.

- **Global Protection.** This is the belief that a government has the right and duty to use its soldiers, sailors, and airmen to protect its citizens anywhere they choose to go, no matter how much risk they choose to take.

- **Interests.** Interests are undefined in law or the Constitution. They are often cited as a reason for the government to get into a war — to protect its "interests."

- **Cost Externalization.** This idea is a complement to global protection and interests. Often a person or a corporation that goes into a high-risk area can persuade the government to "externalize" (shift) the costs of protection onto the taxpayers and onto the government's soldiers, sailors, and airmen.

- **Manifest Destiny.** Originally, this was the belief that God gave the U.S. Government the right to capture and rule all the land from the Atlantic to the Pacific regardless of who might already be living there. After that land was taken, Manifest Destiny was extended to other nations, leading to the Spanish-American War and conquest of the Philippines. Manifest Destiny led to Anglo-Saxonism.

- **The White Man's Burden or Anglo-Saxonism.** This was the belief that English-speaking white Christians of British cultural heritage have the right to conquer "primitive" people for the purpose of uplifting them and civilizing them. This belief has been remade into Washington's Burden, although most of the religious and racial bigotry has been dropped (we hope). Today, Washington's Burden is generally taken to mean that the USG must be a global enforcer. This view was articulated in 1998 by Secretary of State Madeleine Albright, who said, "If we have to use force, it is because we are America. We are the indispensable nation. We stand tall. We see farther into the future."[149]

- **Alliances.** In the belief that there is safety in numbers, governments form alliances; each promises to help the others in time of war. In actual practice, alliances mean, if one of us goes to war

---

[149] BLOWBACK, by Chalmers Johnson, Henry Holt and Company, NY, 2000, p.217.

we all do. So each country's fate is in the hands of all the other governments in the alliance. If one government makes a mistake, or deliberately provokes a war, the alliance produces a domino effect that draws in all the others.

- **The Glory of War.** This refers to the pomp and pageantry — the songs, medals, parades, uniforms, speeches, and other displays that stir the emotions and promise young men (and now young women) the chance to be heroes. The pomp and pageantry work hand in hand with propaganda to destroy a person's judgment.

Chris, if I had to condense all ten ideas into one word, that word would be **hubris.** Hubris means overbearing pride or arrogance. In politics, hubris often leads to the assumption that one is so superior he is entitled to force others to bend to his will.

It reminds me of the warning: "Pride goeth before destruction, and a haughty spirit before a fall."

As you may recall from my earlier letter, Chris, in 2001 the USG was thrown off the United Nation's Human Rights Committee. U.S. officials were told that they were being taught a lesson, not only by their enemies, but also by their allies in Europe who were giving notice that the USG had become too arrogant.

In the nineteenth century, these ten deadly ideas were gradually infused into the American attitude toward the rest of the world through a long sequence of events that included but were not limited to the Barbary Wars, Perry's gunboat diplomacy in Japan, the Spanish-American War, and the conquest of the Philippines. This then led to the USG's entry into the war that began in 1914, turning it into a world war. That world war then led to World War II, the Korean War, Vietnam War, and eventually September 11th and the destruction of the World Trade Center. I will cover these later wars in my next set of letters about the Second World War.

Chris, everyone today knows the First World War happened, but few have much knowledge of it. While researching the ideas and events that produced the war, I often had friends ask, what was the war about?

It was about nothing at all. Old World governments have been fighting for thousands of years. In 1914, under the deadly idea of alliances, Old World powers had promised each other that if one went to war, they all would. When the Serbs and Austrians started shooting at each other, they all did. It was as simple as that. Dominoes.

Summary   **213**

Chris, in a recent letter you asked if I was "against" America's armed forces.

No, of course not. It isn't that we should not have armed forces, it is that we have the wrong kind.

We have the kind designed to "project power," which means get into other people's wars. And our armed forces do this very well. In fact, they have done it so well for so long that on September 11, 2001, the foreign wars they have been sent into followed them home to American soil. You are aware of this because you have read my previous set of letters about this new "War on Terror."[150]

We need the kind of armed forces deemed necessary by the Second Amendment — a "well-regulated militia," trained and equipped with the latest and best weapons, to fight as guerrillas who can make the country impossible for an enemy to occupy, and who can find and kill the enemy's leaders. A defensive force, like a porcupine. This is how we can protect our homeland without meddling in other countries and without being a threat to other countries.

Chris, let me return to a question I asked in one of my first letters. What is patriotism?

Many would say, my country right or wrong.

In actual practice, my country right or wrong means my government right or wrong. In other words, this definition of patriotism leads to doing whatever the government says, even if it is unethical and even if it violates the two fundamental laws taught by all religions — do all you have agreed to do, and do not encroach on other persons or their property.

---

[150] Uncle Eric is referring to Richard J. Maybury's book THE THOUSAND YEAR WAR IN THE MIDEAST: HOW IT AFFECTS YOU TODAY, published by Bluestocking Press, web site: www.BluestockingPress.com

To me, patriotism means dedication to the *principles* on which the country was founded, and a willingness to fight for these principles no matter what the government might say or do.

Now that you know something about the causes of World War I, and the aftermath, which led to World War II, I think you can see why I feel so strongly about this definition of patriotism.

Unfortunately, World War I was a paragon of ethics and good judgment compared to World War II. I will tell you all about it in my next set of letters.[151]

Until then, whenever you see a film, listen to a political speech, or read an article or book, including this one, ask yourself, "What is the writer's agenda? What does he want me to think?"

Someday, Chris, you may be called upon to don a uniform and march off to war. I care about you very much, so I will be as clear and blunt about this as I can.

If fighting to protect your home and family is necessary, then by all means do it.

But, please, Chris, don't ever march off to war until you fully understand the opponent's point of view, and only after you have seen a mountain of evidence that the war is for an extremely good reason. Probably the only good thing that came out of World War I is this lesson.

Uncle Eric

---

[151] Uncle Eric is referring to Richard J. Maybury's book WORLD WAR II: THE REST OF THE STORY, part two in Maybury's World War series, published by Bluestocking Press, web site: www.BluestockingPress.com

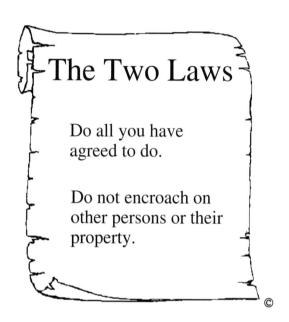

The Two Laws

Do all you have
agreed to do.

Do not encroach on
other persons or their
property.

©

The two laws that make civilization possible.

Spread the Word!

Everything for which America has fought has been accomplished. It will now be our fortunate duty to assist by example, by sober, friendly counsel, and by material aid, in the establishment of just democracy throughout the world.

— Woodrow Wilson
November 11, 1918
upon the surrender of Germany at the end of WWI

The first casualty when war comes is truth.
— Senator Hiram Johnson, 1917

Appendix

The War Prayer
by Mark Twain

*Mark Twain (Samuel Clemens) was a fierce opponent of
America's new imperialism including the wars in Cuba, the
Philippines, and China. He is believed to have written this
short story in 1904 or 1905, but received so much criticism
from editors and others that it was not published until after
his death.*

It was a time of great and exalting excitement. The country
was up in arms, the war was on, in every breast burned the
holy fire of patriotism; the drums were beating, the bands
playing, the toy pistols popping, the bunched firecrackers
hissing and sputtering; on every hand and far down the
receding and fading spread of roofs and balconies a fluttering
wilderness of flags flashed in the sun; daily the young
volunteers marched down the wide avenue gay and fine in
their new uniforms, the proud fathers and mothers and sisters
and sweethearts cheering them with voices choked with
happy emotion as they swung by; nightly the packed mass
meetings listened, panting, to patriot oratory which stirred
the deepest depths of their hearts and which they interrupted
at briefest intervals with cyclones of applause, the tears
running down their cheeks the while; in the churches the
pastors preached devotion to flag and country and invoked
the God of Battles, beseeching His aid in our good cause in
outpouring of fervid eloquence which moved every listener.

It was indeed a glad and gracious time, and the half-dozen
rash spirits that ventured to disapprove of the war and cast a
doubt upon its righteousness straightway got such a stern

and angry warning that for their personal safety's sake they quickly shrank out of sight and offended no more in that way.

Sunday morning came — next day the battalions would leave for the front; the church was filled; the volunteers were there, their young faces alight with martial dreams — visions of the stern advance, the gathering momentum, the rushing charge, the flashing sabers, the flight of the foe, the tumult, the enveloping smoke, the fierce pursuit, the surrender! — then home from the war, bronzed heroes, welcomed, adored, submerged in golden seas of glory!

With the volunteers sat their dear ones, proud, happy, and envied by the neighbors and friends who had no sons and brothers to send forth to the field of honor, there to win for the flag, or failing, die the noblest of noble deaths.

The service proceeded; a war chapter from the Old Testament was read; the first prayer was said; it was followed by an organ burst that shook the building, and with one impulse the house rose, with glowing eyes and beating hearts, and poured out that tremendous invocation — God the all-terrible! Thou who ordainest, Thunder thy clarion and lightning thy sword!

Then came the "long" prayer. None could remember the like of it for passionate pleading and moving and beautiful language. The burden of its supplication was that an ever-merciful and benignant Father of us all would watch over our noble young soldiers and aid, comfort, and encourage them in their patriotic work; bless them, shield them in the day of battle and the hour of peril, bear them in His mighty hand, make them strong and confident, invincible in the bloody onset; help them to crush the foe, grant to them and to flag and country imperishable honor and glory.

An aged stranger entered and moved with slow and noiseless step up the main aisle, his eyes fixed upon the minister, his long body clothed in a robe that reached to his feet, his head bare, his white hair descending in a frothy cataract to his shoulders, his seamy face unnaturally pale, pale even to ghastliness.

With all eyes following him and wondering, he made his silent way; without pausing, he ascended to the preacher's side and stood there waiting.

With shut eyes the preacher, unconscious of his presence, continued his moving prayer, and at last finished it with the words, uttered in fervent appeal, "Bless our arms, grant us the victory, O Lord our God, Father and Protector of our land and flag!"

The stranger touched his arm, motioned him to step aside — which the startled minister did — and took his place.

During some moments he surveyed the spellbound audience with solemn eyes in which burned an uncanny light; then in a deep voice he said: "I come from the throne of Almighty God!"

The words smote the house with a shock; if the stranger perceived it he gave no attention.

"He has heard the prayer of His shepherd and will grant it if such be your desire after I, His messenger, shall have explained to you its import — that is to say, its full import. For it is like unto many of the prayers of men, in that it asks for more than he who utters it is aware of — except he pause and think.

"God's servant and yours has prayed his prayer. Has he paused and taken thought? Is it one prayer? No, it is two — one uttered, the other not. Both have reached the ear of Him Who heareth all supplications, the spoken and the unspoken. Ponder this — keep it in mind.

"If you would beseech a blessing upon yourself, beware! lest without intent you invoke a curse upon a neighbor at the same time.

"If you pray for the blessing of rain upon your crop which needs it, by that act you are possibly praying for a curse upon some neighbor's crop which may not need rain and can be injured by it.

"You have heard your servant's prayer — the uttered part of it. I am commissioned of God to put into words the other part of it — that part which the pastor, and also you in your hearts, fervently prayed silently.

"And ignorantly and unthinkingly? God grant that it was so! You heard these words: 'Grant us the victory, O Lord our God!' That is sufficient. The whole of the uttered prayer is compact into those pregnant words. Elaborations were not necessary.

"When you have prayed for victory you have prayed for many unmentioned results which follow victory — must follow it, cannot help but follow it. Upon the listening spirit of God the Father fell also the unspoken part of the prayer. He commandeth me to put it into words. LISTEN!

"O Lord our Father, our young patriots, idols of our hearts, go forth to battle — be Thou near them!

"With them, in spirit, we also go forth from the sweet peace of our beloved firesides to smite the foe.

"O Lord our God, help us to tear their soldiers to bloody shreds with our shells; help us to cover their smiling fields with the pale forms of their patriot dead; help us to drown the thunder of the guns with the shrieks of their wounded, writhing in pain; help us to lay waste their humble homes with a hurricane of fire; help us to wring the hearts of their unoffending widows with unavailing grief; help us to turn them out roofless with their little children to wander unfriended the wastes of their desolated land in rags and hunger and thirst, sports of the sun flames of summer and the icy winds of winter, broken in spirit, worn with travail, imploring Thee for the refuge of the grave and denied it — for our sakes who adore Thee, Lord, blast their hopes, blight their lives, protract their bitter pilgrimage, make heavy their steps, water their way with their tears, stain the white snow with the blood of their wounded feet!

We ask it, in the spirit of love, of Him Who is the Source of Love, and Who is the ever-faithful refuge and friend of all that are sore beset and seek His aid with humble and contrite hearts. AMEN.

After a pause: "Ye have prayed it; if ye still desire it, speak! The messenger of the Most High waits."

It was believed afterward that the man was a lunatic, because there was no sense in what he said.

Quotes About War

Each of these comments makes a point that can be used for discussion or research. Is the point true, what do you think?

"Injustice, arrogance, displayed in the hour of triumph will never be forgotten or forgiven."

— David Lloyd George
Memo from the World War I surrender conference, 1919

"Against war it may be said that it makes the victor stupid and the vanquished revengeful."

— Friedrich Nietzsche
HUMAN, ALL TOO HUMAN, 1878

"If they want peace, nations should avoid the pinpricks that precede cannon shots."

— Napoleon Bonaparte
Reported conversation with Czar Alexander, 1807

"War involves in its progress such a train of unforeseen and unsupposed circumstances that no human wisdom can calculate the end. It has but one thing certain, and that is to increase taxes."

— Thomas Paine
PROSPECTS ON THE RUBICON, 1787

"Nay, number itself in armies importeth not much, where the people is of weak courage; for as Virgil saith, "It never troubles the wolf how many the sheep be."

— Sir Francis Bacon
"Of The True Greatness of Kingdoms and Estates"
ESSAYS, 1625

"I find war detestable but those who praise it without participating in it even more so."
— Romain Rolland
"Inter arma caritas"
JOURNAL DE GENEVE, 1914

"They may ring their bells now, before long they will be wringing their hands."
— Sir Robert Walpole
Speech about the celebrations in England
at the beginning of a war with Spain, 1739

"They make a desert and call it peace."
— Tacitus
AGRICOLA, circa 98 A.D.

"All wars are wars among thieves who are too cowardly to fight and who therefore induce the young manhood of the whole world to do the fighting for them."
— Emma Goldman
"Address to the Jury"
MOTHER EARTH, 1917

"There is many a boy here today who looks on war as all glory, but, boys, it is all hell."
— William Tecumseh Sherman
Speech in Columbus, Ohio, 1880

"It is not merely cruelty that leads men to love war, it is excitement."
— Henry Ward Beecher
PROVERBS FROM PLYMOUTH PULPIT, 1887

"As long as war is regarded as wicked, it will always have its fascination. When it is looked upon as vulgar, it will cease to be popular."

— Oscar Wilde
INTENTIONS, 1891

"Once blood is shed in a national quarrel, reason and right are swept aside by the rage of angry men."

— David Lloyd George
1933-36

"I tell you there's nothing to stop war from going on forever. ... A slight case of negligence, and it's bogged down up to the axles. And then it's a matter of hauling the war out of the mud again. But emperors and kings and popes will come to its rescue."

— Bertolt Brecht
MOTHER COURAGE, 1939

"Diplomats are just as essential to starting a war as soldiers are for finishing it. You take diplomacy out of war and the thing would fall flat in a week."

— Will Rogers
AUTOBIOGRAPHY OF WILL ROGERS, 1949

"We Smiths want peace so bad we are willing to kill every one of the Joneses to get it."

— I.F. Stone
quoted in the
TRUMAN ERA, 1949

"War is both the product of an earlier corruption and a producer of new corruptions."

— Lewis Mumford
THE CONDUCT OF LIFE, 1951

"Every gun that is fired, every warship launched, every rocket fired signifies, in the final sense, a theft from those who hunger and are not fed, those who are cold and are not clothed. The world in arms is not spending money alone. It is spending the sweat of its laborers, the genius of its scientists, the hopes of its children."

— President Dwight D. Eisenhower
Speech, 1953

"Past experience provides little basis for confidence that reason can prevail in an atmosphere of war fever."

— J. William Fulbright
Speech to U.S. Senate, 1966

"Laws are silent in time of war."

— Cicero
PRO MILONE, 52 B.C.

"A general and a bit of shooting makes you forget your troubles ... it takes your mind off the cost of living."

— Brendan Behan
THE HOSTAGE, 1958

"I believe that the real reason why war exists is because men have always liked war, and women, warriors."

— Martin van Creveld
RISE AND DECLINE OF THE STATE, 1999

"Men love war because it allows them to look serious. Because it is the one thing that stops women laughing at them."
— John Fowles
THE MAGUS, 1965

"There's nothing like a good war to make people feel important."
— Congressional aide quoted in NEWSWEEK
October 10, 1990

"The word state is identical with the word war."
— Prince Peter Kropotkin
PAROLES D'UN REVOLTE, 1885

"We are not about to send American boys nine or ten thousand miles away from home to do what Asian boys ought to be doing for themselves."
— President Lyndon B. Johnson
Speech about the Vietnam War, 1964

"In times of peace the people look most to their representatives; but in war, to the executive solely."
— Thomas Jefferson
Letter to Caesar A. Rodney, 1810

"Everyone, when there's a war in the air, learns to live in a new element: falsehood."
— Jean Giraudoux
TIGER AT THE GATES, 1935

"The Bill of Rights stops at the border."
— Richard Maybury
(Uncle Eric)

Bibliography
and Suggested Reading

- ATLAS OF THE FIRST WORLD WAR by Martin Gilbert, Oxford University Press, NY, 1994

- ATLAS OF RUSSIAN HISTORY by Martin Gilbert, Dorset Press, Great Britain, 1972

- DEATH BY GOVERNMENT by R.J. Rummel, Transaction Publishers, New Brunswick, NJ, 1994

- EMPIRE AS A WAY OF LIFE by William Appleman Williams, Oxford University Press, NY, 1980

Suggested Listening

- THE SPANISH-AMERICAN WAR, Knowledge Products audio history, distributed by Bluestocking Press, Placerville, CA. Ph: 800-959-8586; www.BluestockingPress.com

- WORLD WAR I, Knowledge Products audio history, distributed by Bluestocking Press, web site: www.BluestockingPress.com

- REMEMBRANCE by John McDermott. Music CD which includes several WWI songs, including: And the Band Played Waltzing Matilda, The Green Fields of France, Roses of Picardy, Lili Marlene, Christmas in the Trenches and In Flanders Fields. Highly recommended.

Suggested Viewing

Although movies generally give the government's official view of the World Wars, there are exceptions, and even some of the most statist movies can paint enlightening pictures of real events.

U.S. foreign and military policy today, in the 21ˢᵗ century, is still largely determined by the emotions generated by World War II movies. As I write this, the government and the country as a whole are now led by baby boomers, and the boomers were raised on a steady diet of World War II films. Screen images and music are so powerful they can overwhelm facts.

— *Richard Maybury*

ALL QUIET ON THE WESTERN FRONT. Good example of trench warfare. Excellent story of German soldiers in WWI who were encouraged to fight for the Fatherland and experience the glory of war.

ADVENTURES OF YOUNG INDIANA JONES, CHAPTER 8, THE TRENCHES OF HELL. Good example of trench warfare.

BREAKER MORANT starring Edward Woodward. 1979. Based on a true story. A superbly accurate picture of the British government's use of ethnic cleansing to build the British Empire under the doctrine of Anglo-Saxonism. Also shows how troops and governments are corrupted by anti-guerrilla warfare. Rated PG.

THE COLOR OF WAR. The segment called "Why We Fight" by the History Channel. This is a most revealing look at the thinking of American soldiers, sailors and airmen in World War II. Among other things, the film explains that in 1942 millions of Americans had no dislike of Germans and many admired them. The government had to use extreme propaganda against Germans so that these millions would hate them. This extreme message still colors our view of both World Wars.

GALLIPOLI. A portion of the film shows the disastrous Gallipoli campaign in Turkey during World War I. Perhaps more revealing, however, is the shallow thinking and strong emotions that lead young men (and now women) to march off to war. Much food for thought. Rated PG.

GETTYSBURG starring Tom Berenger shows how lines of men with rifles would rush at each other as they had been doing in Europe for centuries, and did again in World War I. Rated PG.

THE PATRIOT starring Mel Gibson. Another depiction of young men with rifles rushing at each other. But more, shows the effectiveness of guerrilla warfare.

SANDS OF IWO JIMA (1949). When marine trainees in 1961 at Camp Pendleton were asked why they had enlisted, half said it was because they had been inspired by SANDS OF IWO JIMA.

THEY WERE EXPENDABLE (1945) starring John Wayne. This is a classic World War II propaganda film aimed at the hearts and minds of young men.

THE UGLY AMERICAN starring Marlon Brando as the American Ambassador to an Asian country. Shows U.S. power struggle.

VICTORY AT SEA. The 1954 television series produced by Henry Salomon. This is another film series that gives the government's side of the story about World War II. If you do not have the time to watch all 26 segments, they have been compressed into a two-hour movie often shown on television. Like WHY WE FIGHT, the VICTORY AT SEA television series is a must.

WHY WE FIGHT directed by Frank Capra. In World War II, the Federal Government wanted a series of films that would explain why Americans should support the fight. The result was the series WHY WE FIGHT which was so persuasive that it became the unquestioned explanation of *both* World Wars. This film will give you a quick yet profound understanding of why Americans believe what they do about the World Wars. Highly recommended.

Glossary

(Other names can be found in the Cast of Characters.)

ALLIANCES. When two or more governments stand together against a common enemy and for a common cause.

ALLIES. In World War I, the alliance led by London, Moscow and Washington; enemies of the Central Powers. In World War II, the same group; enemies of the Axis.

ANGLO-SAXONISM. The White Man's Burden. The belief that the U.S. and British governments have the right to conquer other nations, especially dark-skinned non-Christians. The term Anglo-Saxon generally refers to English speaking whites of British cultural descent.

ANTI-FEDERALIST. One who opposed creation of the Federal Government. An example was Patrick Henry.

AREA BOMBING. A British term from World War II. The bombing of civilian housing areas for the purpose of killing and terrorizing civilian men, women, and children. Done mostly by the British to Germans, but also done to some extent by Americans to Germans, and to a greater extent by Americans to Japanese.

ARYAN RACE. A Nazi propaganda term meaning a Nordic Caucasian of non-Jewish descent.

AXIS. In World War II, the alliance led by Berlin, Rome, and Tokyo. Enemies of the Allies.

BARBARIAN. A person with a civilization regarded as primitive. A hazy term, barbarian was originally an ancient Roman word for northern Europeans who were not Roman.

BATTALION. In the infantry, about 800 troops. Typically but not always there are nine troops in a squad, three squads to a platoon, four platoons to a company, six companies to a battalion, two battalions to a brigade, and six brigades to a division.

CARPET BOMBING. Means large numbers of planes laying a carpet of bombs across the target.

CENTRAL POWERS. In World War I, the group led by Germany and Austria-Hungary. Consisted of Germany, the Austro-Hungarian Empire, Turkey and Bulgaria. Enemies of the Allies.

COSSACKS. An ethnic group located mostly in southern Russia. Militantly Christian, Cossacks were "the sword arm of the Czars" against the Turks (Muslims), and against anyone who rebelled against the Czars.

COST EXTERNALIZATION. Shifting costs onto someone who does not get the benefits. Usually done covertly.

DELAYED STRESS SYNDROME. An emotional illness caused by the stress of combat. In World War I, called shell shock. In World War II, battle fatigue.

DIPLOMACY. Communication and negotiations between governments.

DIVISION. Generally, six brigades. An infantry division is about 10,000 troops. An armored division, about 600 tanks. Typically but not always there are nine troops in a squad, three squads to a platoon, four platoons to a company, six companies to a battalion, two battalions to a brigade, and six brigades to a division.

ECONOMICS. The study of the production and distribution of goods and services.

FACTION. A small group or subgroup within a larger group.

FASCES. A bundle of rods bound with an ax or spear. The bound rods symbolized all the people of all the provinces "unified" under a single government. The ax or spear symbolized what happened to anyone who did not obey this government.

FASCISM. The political philosophy that is no philosophy at all. Do whatever appears necessary. It is derived from the law of the Roman Empire.

FEDERALIST. One who advocated a strong central government for the U.S. An example was Alexander Hamilton.

FOREIGN POLICY. The government's behavior toward other governments and toward persons in other lands.

FRAGGING. Tossing a fragmentation grenade into an officer's tent by one of his own men. Also used more generally to refer to any means of killing a higher ranking person.

FUNGIBLE. Each unit is indistinguishable from another, so each can substitute for another.

GEOPOLITICAL. World political events, as opposed to national political events.

GLOBAL PROTECTION. The belief that a government has the right and duty to use its soldiers, sailors, and airmen to protect its citizens anywhere they choose to go, no matter how much risk they choose to take.

GREAT WAR. The original name for the First World War. Abandoned after the Second World War.

GUNBOAT DIPLOMACY. Using military force to frighten foreigners into signing agreements.

HOHENZOLLERN. The ruling family of Prussia and Germany.

HUBRIS. Means overbearing pride or arrogance. In politics, hubris often leads to the assumption that one is so superior he is entitled to force others to bend to his will.

IMPERIALISTS. One who wishes to conquer others and force them into his empire.

INTERESTS. Interests are undefined in law or the Constitution. They are often cited as a reason for the government to get into a war — to protect its interests.

ISOLATIONISM. Having no political or economic relations of any kind with other countries.

KREMLIN. A medieval fortified area in Moscow used as the center of the Russian government. The word is commonly used to mean the Russian government.

KULTUR. (pronounced cool-tour) German culture and civilization. Used in U.S. propaganda to mean the German mind, the thinking of all Germans.

LEAGUE OF NATIONS. Predecessor of the United Nations; the first attempt to create a world government. The failure of the League of Nations to stop Italy's invasion of Ethiopia is often cited as a cause of World War II. Many Americans bemoan the loss of the League and the incompetence of the United Nations because they believe a single world government that can force its will onto anyone, anywhere, is the way to create peace and liberty for all.

LEBENSRAUM. German for living space. The reason Hitler launched his attack on the U.S.S.R, to capture land for Germans to expand into.

MAMELUKES. A military group originally composed of slaves from Turkey. They ruled Egypt from about 1250 until 1517, and remained powerful there until 1811.

MANIFEST DESTINY. The belief that God gave the U.S. Government the right to capture and rule all the land from the Atlantic to the Pacific.

MOBILIZE or **MOBILIZATION.** To prepare for war, especially to move forces in the direction of the enemy, but not to cross onto their soil. Crossing onto to their soil is the next step, invasion.

NATIONALISM. Intense devotion to one's nation; intense patriotism.

NEUTRALITY. Not aligned with, supporting, or favoring any side in a war or dispute.

NONINTERVENTION. Similar to neutrality. Refusal to meddle in the affairs of another nation, or in a dispute or war.

NON-STATIST. One who believes there is a higher law than any human law, and the government should be subject to this law and kept very limited.

OBJECTIVE. Opposite of subjective. Having to do with a real object rather than an opinion. Being independent of the mind; real, actual, existing.

OCCUPATION. Seizure and control of an area by military forces.

OCCUPY. To station troops in a country to watch the conquered people and force them to obey the laws of the conqueror.

PATRIOTISM. Dedication to the *principles* on which the country was founded, and a willingness to stand firm and fight for these principles regardless of what the government says or does.

PAX ROMANA. The two centuries starting in 31 B.C. usually assumed to be a period of peace in the Roman Empire.

POLITICAL POWER. The legal privilege of using force on persons who have not harmed anyone. The privilege of backing one's decisions with violence or threats of violence. This privilege is what sets government apart from all other institutions.

PROPAGANDA. Strongly biased information designed to persuade, usually relating to political or economic matters. The bias is often subtle and usually hidden, and may make use of lies and half-truths.

REPARATIONS. Money, land or goods forced from a defeated nation as compensation for damage or injury during a war.

STATIST. One who believes in a large, powerful central government, and who believes that there is no law higher than the government's law.

SUBJECTIVE. Opposite of objective. Having to do with opinion rather than actual fact. Affected by the feelings or beliefs of the observer.

TAKE NO PRISONERS. Kill everyone, even those who try to surrender.

TRENCH SWEEPERS. A small, portable machine gun.

VICTORIAN ERA. When Queen Victoria reigned in England, 1837 to 1901.

WAR FEVER. An intense desire for war.

WHITE MAN'S BURDEN. Anglo-Saxonism. The belief that the U.S. Goverment and British government have the right to conquer other nations, especially dark-skinned non-Christians.

YIHEQUAN. A Chinese guerrilla group that fought the Boxer Rebellion against foreign powers. Means righteous and harmonious fists.

About Richard J. Maybury

Richard Maybury, also known as Uncle Eric, is a world renowned author, lecturer and geopolitical analyst. He consults with business firms in the U.S. and Europe. Richard is the former Global Affairs editor of MONEYWORLD and widely regarded as one of the finest free-market writers in America. Mr. Maybury's articles have appeared in THE WALL STREET JOURNAL, USA TODAY, and other major publications.

During the 1960s, in the U.S. Air Force 605th Air Commando Squadron, Mr. Maybury was an aircrew member on AC-47, C-47 and C-46 aircraft, and was involved in covert warfare operations in Central America. He saw, in his own words, "real politics, up front and personal, and it isn't anything like what most Americans think it is."

Richard Maybury has penned eleven books in the Uncle Eric series. His books have been endorsed by top business leaders including former U.S. Treasury Secretary William Simon, and he has been interviewed on more than 250 radio and TV shows across America.

He has been married for more than 35 years, has lived abroad, traveled around the world, and visited 48 states and 40 countries.

He is truly a teacher for all ages.

Index

I

J

K

"...the entire [Uncle Eric] series should be a required, integral, component of the social studies curriculum in all public and private schools. This would bring a quantum leap upward in the quality of citizenship in this country in a single generation."

—William P. Snavely
Emeritus Professor of Economics
George Mason University

Study Guides and / or Tests available (or forthcoming)

for the Uncle Eric books

Each study guide will include some, and at times all, of the following:

1) Chapter-by-chapter comprehension questions

2) Research activities

3) A list of films

4) Thought questions

5) Final exam

Order from your favorite book store or direct from the publisher:

Bluestocking Press
www.BluestockingPress.com

(See contact information
on the last page of this book.)

"Uncle Eric is on my top 10 list of homeschool resources."

—William Cormier
Freelance Writer for homeschool publications

"None of my kids are graduating from high school until they've finished reading all these books. Very highly recommended." (5 hearts)

— Mary Pride, PRACTICAL HOMESCHOOLING MAGAZINE

Bluestocking Press

Bluestocking Press publishes the following:

1) Richard J. Maybury's Uncle Eric books (and the accompanying student study guides for the Uncle Eric books)

2) Karl Hess' CAPITALISM FOR KIDS

3) Kathryn Daniels' COMMON SENSE BUSINESS FOR KIDS

4) ECONOMICS: A FREE MARKET READER

5) LAURA INGALLS WILDER AND ROSE WILDER LANE HISTORICAL TIMETABLE

Visit the BLUESTOCKING PRESS CATALOG online at
www.BluestockingPress.com

To order by phone, contact Bluestocking Press
(See contact information
on the last page of this book.)

Published by Bluestocking Press

Uncle Eric Books by Richard J. Maybury

UNCLE ERIC TALKS ABOUT PERSONAL, CAREER, AND FINANCIAL SECURITY

WHATEVER HAPPENED TO PENNY CANDY?

WHATEVER HAPPENED TO JUSTICE?

ARE YOU LIBERAL? CONSERVATIVE? OR CONFUSED?

ANCIENT ROME: HOW IT AFFECTS YOU TODAY

EVALUATING BOOKS: WHAT WOULD THOMAS JEFFERSON THINK ABOUT THIS?

THE MONEY MYSTERY

THE CLIPPER SHIP STRATEGY

THE THOUSAND YEAR WAR IN THE MIDEAST

WORLD WAR I: THE REST OF THE STORY

WORLD WAR II: THE REST OF THE STORY

Bluestocking Guides (study guides for the Uncle Eric books)
by Jane A. Williams and/or Kathryn Daniels

Each Study Guide includes some or all of the following:

1) chapter-by-chapter comprehension questions and answers
2) application questions and answers
3) research activities
4) essay assignments
5) thought questions
6) final exam

More Bluestocking Press Titles

LAURA INGALLS WILDER AND ROSE WILDER LANE HISTORICAL TIMETABLE

CAPITALISM FOR KIDS: GROWING UP TO BE YOUR OWN BOSS by Karl Hess

COMMON SENSE BUSINESS FOR KIDS by Kathryn Daniels

ECONOMICS: A FREE MARKET READER edited by Jane Williams & Kathryn Daniels

Order information: Order any of the above by phone or online from:

Bluestocking Press
Phone: 800-959-8586
email: CustomerService@BluestockingPress.com
web site: www.BluestockingPress.com